R.E.D.S.

REFORMED, EXEGETICAL AND DOCTRINAL STUDIES

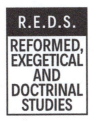

CLASH
OF VISIONS

POPULISM AND ELITISM IN NEW TESTAMENT THEOLOGY

ROBERT W. YARBROUGH

SERIES EDITORS J.V. FESKO & MATTHEW BARRETT

MENTOR
Encouraging Christians to Think

Copyright © Robert Yarbrough 2019

paperback ISBN 978-1-5271-0391-7
epub ISBN 978-1-5271-0455-6
mobi ISBN 978-1-5271-0456-3

10 9 8 7 6 5 4 3 2 1

Published in 2019
in the
Mentor Imprint
by
Christian Focus Publications Ltd,
Geanies House, Fearn, Ross-shire,
IV20 1TW, Great Britain.

www.christianfocus.com

Cover design
by Pete Barnsley

Printed by
Bell & Bain, Glasgow

In this short little book, Prof. Robert Yarbrough argues what should be obvious to many but is not, namely, that the New Testament is a religious book and is therefore of interest to religious people. It is not a text to be endlessly compared, dissected, or deconstructed for the amusement of elites or to provide them with assurance that they need not take God too seriously. To the contrary, Yarbrough shows that the majority of Christians in the majority world are interested in the theological and spiritual dimension of the Bible and that is a legitimate way of reading a book like the Bible. While Yarbrough can be questioned on points, his basic thesis holds: the Bible is the church's book.

MICHAEL F. BIRD
Academic Dean and Lecturer in Theology,
Ridley College, Melbourne, Australia

Based on his expertise in the history of New Testament scholarship and in commentary writing, Professor Robert Yarbrough here summarizes his views on the most important questions of biblical scholarship: With which methods, with which views on Scripture do we approach the Bible? What we shall find in it, whether it can help our life here on earth and in eternity will depend on our hermeneutical decisions. Professor Yarbrough presents many examples of two 'clashing' approaches – but only one of them has the fruit of leading and strengthening readers of Scripture to finding and following Christ as their Savior. Christianity is growing in places where people read Scripture with openness to its own claims and not as judges over it. There is hope for future Christendom, and also for mission, if Jesus is the center of Scripture and of the life of its readers.

PÉTER BALLA
Rector, Károli Gáspár University of the
Reformed Church in Hungary

Bob Yarbrough's book, *Clash of Visions*, is a breath of fresh air in the midst of the theological pollution of liberal Christianity that persists in the Western world. The book contrasts the liberal 'elitists' and the Christian 'populists.' The former have denied the supernatural in the Bible, while the latter believe it (e.g., Christ's deity, the virgin birth, Christ's miracles, the inerrancy of the Bible, the penal substitutionary death of Jesus, and the resurrection of Christ). At the beginning of the book Yarbrough narrates a debate between a classic 'elitist' theologian (formerly educated at Wheaton College and who studied under Yarbrough himself) and a 'populist,' both of whom teach at the same state university in Sweden. The debate between these two theologians provides an excellent window through which the contrasting perspectives can be seen. Anyone who has studied biblical studies or theology at a non-evangelical university or seminary (as I have) will immediately identify and appreciate this book. The 'elitists' rarely welcome viewpoints that oppose their view and make those who disagree with them feel stupid. Yarbrough, indeed, shows that it is the 'elitists' that are out step with historic Christianity, which goes all the way back to the Apostles. The book provides perspective, showing that 'elitist' theology is losing its impact on the Christian movement around the world, while 'populism,' i.e., Bible-believing Christianity, is spreading like wildfire around the world (especially in Latin America and Africa). This is a book that every Christian student should read before studying at a non-evangelical institution. Even those at Bible-believing institutions (including seminaries) will benefit, since they will likely be reading books by 'elitists' and may at some point study under them in graduate school. I found the book riveting and had a hard time putting it down. The two appendices about the life-pilgrimage of two 'populist' theologians alone are worth the price of the book.

G. K. BEALE
J. Gresham Machen Chair and Research Professor of New Testament
and Biblical Theology, Westminster Theological Seminary,
Philadelphia, Pennsylvania

Clash of Visions is, in turn, prophetic and pastoral, polemic and irenic, disturbing and encouraging, scholarly and lay-accessible. Yarbrough contrasts millions of spiritually-vital, Bible-believing, even 'martyr-brave' populists with the dreary but influential platoon of Baur/Bultmann enthusiasts, the guild of elitists who've fallen into the 'ugly wide ditch' of historiocriticalism. He employs a cast of hundreds in both vintage and contemporary garb, quotes old hymns and Tom Petty songs as well as Werke besotted by Aufklärung, and coins expressions ('neo-allegorical') as he appropriates others ('human ecology'). The testimonies are compelling, as is a photo of contrasting grave markers. A great read.

MARK COPPENGER
Professor of Christian Philosophy and Ethics,
Southern Baptist Theological Seminary

CONTENTS

Introduction

A first order of business is to clarify terms paired in this book's subtitle: 'populism' and 'elitism'. Careful definitions and qualifications emerge as the book proceeds. For now, it is important only to stress that neither word has any connection with contemporary political figures like Donald Trump (regarded by many as a populist leader in the pejorative sense) or his opponents. This is not a book about political convictions or movements. It is rather an analysis of hermeneutical outlooks affecting how the New Testament is read and synthesized in two contrasting domains, conceptually and geographically: one in which the church tends to be stagnant or receding, the other in which the largest numeric increase of professing Christians in world history has been underway for several generations and is projected to continue.

That matter aside, lying behind this brief study is a two-fold impetus.

1. Occasion

First, there was an invitation to deliver the Gheens Lectures at The Southern Baptist Theological Seminary in Louisville, Kentucky on February 27 and 28, 2018. The three chapters of this book are basically those lectures. There has been some fleshing out of footnotes and occasional alteration or expansion elsewhere. The two appendices, for example, were not part of the lectures. Otherwise changes, while significant, have not been extensive.

I am grateful to the administration and faculty of that historic seminary for the opportunity to explore the topic I eventually settled on for this occasion and audience. In addition to Dr R. Albert Mohler, Jr, President, whose office extended the invitation, special thanks are due to those most extensively engaged in arrangements and hospitality: Dr Gregory A. Wills, Dean, School of Theology; and then professors Dr Jonathan Pennington, Dr Daniel Gurtner, Dr Mark Coppenger, Dr Thomas Schreiner, and Dr Brian Vickers. Also, in the thick of logistics were Mrs Elizabeth McCulley, Senior Administrative Assistant to the Dean, and Trey Moss, Assistant to the Director of Research Doctoral Studies. Mr Moss was also involved in arranging a delightful afternoon with the weekly doctoral seminar attended by several dozen students. I offer my sincere thanks to all.

2. Field of Inquiry

Second, given over thirty years of involvement in teaching New Testament and related subjects (i.e., Hellenistic Greek, Septuagint, history of interpretation), and given my particular interest in the rise and development (especially in Germany) of contemporary New Testament interpretation,[1] I was drawn to a study that would center on issues and major figures in that enterprise. A spirited published exchange between two scholars at Uppsala University captured key elements of the tension I wished to explore. That interchange became the core of chapter one, which contrasts so-called 'critical' interpretation of the New Testament with what may be termed 'confessional' reading. In terms of this book's title, 'critical' too often assumes the form of an 'elitist' orientation, while 'confessional' often aligns with 'populist'.

The term 'elitist' is appropriate in that 'critical' (short for 'historical critical') interpretation is primarily the domain of a relatively small group of highly trained scholars who in many cases do not regard the Bible as the divinely-given writings that most Christians in most places

---

1. See my *The Salvation Historical Fallacy? Rethinking the History of New Testament Theology* (Leiden: Deo, 2004).

and times have regarded the Scriptures to be. Accordingly, they question the accuracy of any number of representations made in the documents, and they disparage readings of those documents that do not comport with 'critical' convention. This disparagement is on full display in chapter one.

'Populist' is likewise appropriate, because in forms described below it rejects the necessity of elite intervention to understand Scripture's message sufficiently to be saved by Christ whose story it conveys. 'Populist' refers to an approach to Scripture that is informal (not tightly regimented), unshackled by too-stringent scholarly conventions and methods (though as chapter one shows 'populist' scholars may well affirm and practice those conventions and methods in the professional guild setting), and open to viewing biblical writings in the light of the dogmatic truths ecclesial readers have tended to find there through the centuries.

'Populist' is also fitting in light of the world church situation, in which numbers of Christian believers have exploded in recent generations. They are apt to read the Bible in 'populist' fashion, meaning they find the truth of Christian doctrine affirmed in the 'historical' documents the Bible contains. 'Elitist' reading, in contrast, often denies saving efficacy, or accuracy, or even relevance to the biblical writings. They may be worth 'critical' scrutiny, but given typical 'critical' assumptions about human nature, Scripture, and God, they do not constitute the authoritative testimony to the salvation Jesus offers to those who accept Scripture as God's Word (conceding at the same time that they reflect, by both historical necessity and divine design, a hefty human component).

While chapter one describes and dramatizes the tension between populist and elitist vantage points, chapter two explores how scholarship is currently revisiting, and often reaffirming, elitist approaches to New Testament theology that many believed had been put to rest generations ago. The scholars highlighted are F. C. Baur (1792–1860) and Rudolf Bultmann (1884–1976). Elitist rendition of New Testament theology, then, far from weakening or moderating after major figures in the tradition (like Baur and Bultmann) were weighed and found wanting in past generations, is making a comeback in some quarters.

Chapter three takes up the question of how elitist and populist views do or do not connect or inter-relate. It is not the goal or intention of populist hermeneutics to thwart or eliminate elitist approaches. It is however the populist goal and intention to draw on the best of all careful and informed scrutiny of the New Testament, untrammeled by elitism's sometimes covert ground rules, which if followed would go far toward eliminating the possibility and necessity of a personal confession of faith in the crucified-yet-risen Savior. Elitist reading would also eliminate the 'high' view of Scripture that has characterized populist church understanding and been instrumental in meteoric church expansion and growth worldwide in recent decades. Chapter three explores some six ways in which populist reading holds out hope for fruitful understanding of Scripture, for personal and communal appropriation of its message, and for continuing progress in investigation of the New Testament writings, their language, their history, their background and cultural setting, and much besides.

The final appendix illustrates how a conversion from rejection of the Bible's message to internalization of it holds potential for fundamental changes in social consciousness and acceptance of those we innately regard as 'other', and commitment to a life of love and service for the sake of other people and God's glory.

3. The Perennial Issue and the Hope

While the historical conditions peculiar to Europe and the rise of historical criticism are novel in many ways, human nature and its social effects display constant or at least recurring features through the centuries. There are uncanny resemblances between the two groups alluded to in this study and two groups hailing from Jesus' own times described by Chris Keith in his book *Jesus Against the Scribal Elite: The Origins of the Conflict*.[2] One group, highly trained in what Keith calls scribal literacy, constituted an authoritative hegemony that resisted challenges from outside their own conventions and ranks. Jesus came into their crosshairs, not because He displayed no wisdom, poise, or insight, but because His (lack of formal) training, maverick (by their lights) hermeneutics, and social location encouraged dismissal of His contentions by the elite. How could a manual laborer lacking formal

2. Grand Rapids: Baker Academic, 2014.

scribal training be correct against the consensus of learned conviction that gradually galvanized in opposition to Him?

One should not romanticize lack of learning. There are evils in populism deserving note. For example, 'income of global foreign missions' is currently estimated at sixty billion dollars.[3] Communities zealous for 'global foreign missions' are presumably of more confessional conviction than are the elite. But outstripping 'income of global foreign missions' in 2019 is money lost to 'ecclesiastical crime', defined as 'amounts embezzled by top custodians of Christian monies'. During 2019, sixty-eight billion dollars are being siphoned off by church graft. Too much of this will take place under populist auspices. There are no perfect communities of biblical hermeneutics; and having the better hermeneutic is no guarantee of righteousness in living it out.

Yet if we may point out evils to which (say) missiologically zealous populists are subject, we may also caution against tendencies of the elite. Daniel J. Mahoney has written tellingly in *The Idol of Our Age: How the Religion of Humanity Subverts Christianity* of 'global elites' who 'do not see any need for the grace of which the Church is the indispensable sacramental instrument'.[4] More broadly, too many place 'faith in the capacity of an elite of international technocrats to govern the world'.[5] This is in the realm of political philosophy, not biblical interpretation. But elites in both domains downplay or rule out transcendent considerations that are at the heart of Christian teaching and the experience of God that can grow forth from that teaching.

As will emerge below, while elite conviction generally correlates with regions of Protestant church decline, in areas of populist faith Christian numbers are surging upward. One new tool for taking the measure of developments, for example, is *Christian Reflection in Africa*.[6] This tome of nearly eight hundred pages contains twelve hundred abstracts of books and articles shedding light on the meteoric expansion of churches in Africa in the past thirty years.

---

3. Statistics in the paragraph are from Todd M. Johnson, Gina A. Zurlo, Albert W. Hickman, and Peter Crossing, 'Christianity 2019: What's Missing? A Call for Further Research,' *International Bulletin of Missionary Research* 43/1 (January 2019) 98.

4. New York/London: Encounter Books, 2018, p. 15.

5. Ibid., p. 97.

6. Paul Bowers, ed. (Carlisle, U.K.: Langham Global Library, 2018).

Research in other areas appears at a rapid rate: to take just one example, there is the 2018 Middlesex University PhD thesis (supervised at London School of Theology) by Darren Carlson: 'Christian Faith and Practice Amongst Migrants in Athens, Greece.' The thesis abstract describes this work as

> the first major study of migrant faith communities and refugee centers conducted in Athens. The study traces the travel stories of participants as they leave their home countries and migrate to Athens. It discusses the ways Christians served migrants along their journey, the ways specific refugee centers served and proclaimed the gospel, and the impact Christian witness had on migrants who were not Christians. The study discusses the reasons participants from a Muslim background gave for converting to Christian faith, and the struggles new believers experienced as they found themselves in a new community of faith. This research adds to a growing literature of conversion amongst migrants, particularly Muslims, who report supernatural dreams as part of their conversion experience. Finally, this study examines eight specific faith communities, made up of Afghans, Persians, Eritreans, Ghanaians, Europeans, Americans, and Greeks, discussing the ways they formed and their unique distinctives.[7]

The Bible – read in populist not elite fashion – is key in this research report. This becomes clear especially in sections like 'Reading or Studying the Bible'.[8] Admittedly the Bible's power is often activated by those who know and live it, as the following incident illustrates. But observe also the force of just a portion of one Johannine verse (3:16):

> A Greek pastor found the love of God to be the most compelling way to share the Christian faith with Muslim refugees. One day a group of men appeared at his ministry center to talk:
> So I closed the door and they asked me, 'You know, we are Muslim?' And I said, 'Ok. What can I do for you?' He said, 'What do you feel about the Koran?' And I said, 'I don't know. I know one thing, that God loves you: For God so loved the world that he gave his only begotten Son.' A few of them began to cry. And they said, 'We never heard that concept talked about.'

---

7. Darren Carlson, 'Christian Faith and Practice Amongst Migrants in Athens, Greece,' PhD thesis, Middlesex University, 2018, ii.

8. Ibid., pp. 154-6.

The Greek missionary had not read the Koran. He had no cultural training in how to reach Muslims. The Muslims knew about the Greek missionary from other Muslims who had been fed and clothed by him; they wanted to understand why. As a result, all of the men began attending a Bible study, confessed Jesus as Lord, and were baptized.[9]

Despite elites and populists at loggerheads in too many quarters, there is hope. 'The word of God is not bound!' (2 Tim. 2:9 ESV). May this book be a fresh avenue for realization of that exclamation.

9. Ibid., pp. 153-4.

CHAPTER ONE

The Enduring 'Critical' Objection to 'Confessional' Reading of Scripture

1. The Shape of the Issue

The topic I wish to tackle is perhaps the biggest elephant in the room when it comes to the sort of graduate-level academic study of Scripture, theology, and related subjects conducted at seminaries which aim to equip ministers of the Word for service in churches whose members regard the Bible to be true. (What 'true' means here will emerge in the discussion below.)

Undergirding graduate-level academic study of Scripture in most[1] of these seminaries is what we may call the guild. Actually, in the guild's view they establish the rules and set the tone for such study. I'm talking about professors of Old Testament, New Testament, and related subjects who populate graduate school and seminary faculties around the world. These are the world's elite biblical studies authorities, in their view; and to the extent authority means degrees, training, and influence, they are correct. To confirm the self-aware existence of this society, some of its distinctives, and its prospects, the book by Stephen D. Moore

---

1. Some esteem lightly the academic study of Scripture. But most are staffed with professors who have earned doctorates from internationally recognized universities or analogous theological graduate schools. Professors trained at that level tend to value the learning they have received, are grateful for how it can enhance both faith and understanding, and seek to instill (confessionally-friendly) academic expertise in their students.

and Yvonne Sherwood, *The Invention of the Biblical Scholar: A Critical Manifesto* is useful.[2]

For most active Christians worldwide and especially in persecuted lands, the Bible is regarded as true when it speaks of matters like

1. a transcendent creator God
2. the Trinity
3. human and cosmic fallen-ness
4. the incarnation
5. the divinity of Christ
6. Christ's virgin birth, atoning death, and bodily resurrection
7. biblical miracles
8. the new birth through renewal by the Holy Spirit as the gospel is preached and received
9. the glorious visible and bodily return of Jesus Christ
10. eternal life and eternal punishment
11. an inspired authoritative Scripture that affirms all these things and much more.

In contrast, a large number of university professors who teach in biblical and theological areas, and many who teach in seminaries, regard the Bible quite differently.

For this elite, the Bible is not, as the church has historically confessed, God's unerring holy Word leading sinners to salvation and offering the world either redemption through faith or judgment due to unbelief. It is rather a random collection of disparate texts no more revelatory of God than other texts associated with other religions. That is why something like (what came to be called) historical criticism of biblical texts is needed: to probe behind the texts to see what really gave them rise, what caused writers to write so extensively and deeply about events and convictions that the hegemonic 'we' of post-Enlightenment scholars knows can never have taken place or been true.

Yet in many ways it is this guild that sets the agenda, even in seminary settings where the Bible is affirmed to be 'true' (see above), for how biblical and theological studies proceed. Guild priorities go

---

2. Minneapolis: Fortress, 2011.

far toward determining what is significant for ministerial students to be aware of and interact with in their training and as they prepare to minister subsequent to graduation. And this is not all bad. Scholars who take a dim view of historic Christianity can still produce scholarship valuable to those who do not. The lexicographical work of Walter Bauer (1877–1960) enshrined in the standard New Testament Greek lexicon serves as an example.[3] We may give thanks for God's common grace in the form of solid academic work from any and all quarters.[4]

Yet the fact that Walter Bauer also wrote the book translated as *Orthodoxy and Heresy in Earliest Christianity* (1934; ET 1971), a study that did much to refine and advance the notion that heresy preceded orthodoxy in early Christianity, and that 'orthodoxy' is a Hellenistic and Roman imposition on the primitive ethical and spiritual movement Jesus actually founded, until Paul and others distorted it, is a reminder of the unhelpful, because erroneous, claims often advanced by post-confessional scholars.[5] It cannot be helpful, either, that dealing with their erroneous claims must so often consume the classroom and research time of students in theological training where the Bible is believed. I'm not saying it isn't necessary: it is, at least in many locations. But I am saying the expenditure of time to absorb and respond to non-believing scholarly explanations of the New Testament is lamentable and sometimes destructive, in that not all students (or professors[6]) emerge

---

3. Reference here is to Bauer's *A Greek-English Lexicon of the New Testament and Other Early Christian Literature*, ed. Frederick William Danker, 3rd edition (Chicago and London: The University of Chicago Press, 2000), commonly cited as BDAG.

4. For a commendation of biblical scholarship in general see Craig Blomberg, 'A Constructive Traditional Response to New Testament Criticism,' in James K. Hoffmeier and Dennis R. Magary, eds., *Do Historical Matters Matter for Faith? A Critical Appraisal of Modern and Postmodern Approaches to Scripture* (Wheaton: Crossway, 2012), pp. 345-65.

5. For a book that exemplifies Bauer's approach, see Elaine Pagels, *Beyond Belief: The Secret Gospel of Thomas* (New York: Random House, 2003). Bauer's thesis also informs much of the work of Bart Ehrman. For analysis of the Bauer thesis that heresy preceded orthodoxy, see Paul A. Hartog, ed., *Orthodoxy and Heresy in Early Christian Contexts: Reconsidering the Bauer Thesis* (Eugene, OR: Pickwick, 2015); Andreas J. Köstenberger and Michael J. Kruger, *The Heresy of Orthodoxy: How Contemporary Culture's Fascination with Diversity Has Reshaped Our Understanding of Early Christianity* (Wheaton: Crossway, 2010).

6. For how scholarship has sometimes negatively affected the faith of those who pursue it, see Robert Yarbrough, '*God's Word in Human Words*: Form-Critical Reflections,' in Hoffmeier and Magary, eds., *Do Historical Matters Matter for Faith?*, pp. 327-43.

from interaction with so-called critical scholarship with their faith and healthy reason intact.

There's another downside to it: the more time and attention we pour into *de facto* veneration of the canonical figures of Western so-called critical scholarship and their theories, the deeper the impression is among our students that this is where the truth lies, in learning and then maybe qualifying the grand theories of each generation's dominant post-confessional thinkers. The more energy we devote to internalizing and then correcting the mistaken claims about the Bible that abound in (especially) Western settings (though they are encountered worldwide), the more many of our students are confirmed in the biblical illiteracy that our society and even our churches seem to foster nowadays, because there is less time left in the curriculum for teaching and learning the Scriptures themselves rather than so-called critical theories about the Scriptures.

All this sheds light on what I mean by 'elitism in New Testament theology'. I will say more about this below, but I have in mind the enterprise that bloomed in the German Enlightenment (with a pre-history long before then). This approach to the New Testament took its bearings especially from G. E. Lessing (1729–1781) and Immanuel Kant (1724–1804), and then F. C. Baur (1792–1860) and the Tübingen school, and later the history of religion school, and eventually the grand synthesis of New Testament conviction presented by Rudolf Bultmann.[7] From this movement have arisen scores of books entitled 'theology of the New Testament' or the like, particularly in Germany, and studies contributing to a synthetic grasp of the whole of New Testament teaching, history, and sometimes both.

New Testament theology as understood by the academic elite, while it has taken many forms over the last two centuries, has always been in agreement that key theological claims advanced in the New Testament, if you just pick it up and read it, are mistaken. Theological training, accordingly, to a large extent involves learning what might and may be said regarding the New Testament given that so much of its own testimony cannot be taken at face value.

---

7. For dozens of valuable primary source readings stretching from Luther to Bultmann and beyond, see Joachim Cochlovius and Peter Zimmerling, eds., *Evangelische Schriftauslegung: Ein Quellen- und Arbeitsbuch für Studium und Gemeinde* (Krelingen: Geistliches Rüstzentrum/Wuppertal: R. Brockhaus, 1987).

As for 'populism' in New Testament theology, I have already listed above nearly a dozen typical convictions of people belonging to this demographic, which I would argue goes all the way back to the first century, unlike the elitist view which by its own reckoning only began with the rejection of populist reading in modern Europe. I'll say more in the next section about populism, but at the academic level we can point to synthetic assessments of the New Testament like those produced in recent generations by George Ladd, Donald Guthrie, I. Howard Marshall, Frank Thielman, Thomas Schreiner, Ben Witherington III, and Craig Blomberg.[8] More broadly, I have in mind the body of convictions that characterize communities that affirm the high view of Scripture that these evangelical scholars along with many others hold to. Today we must speak immediately of the now hundreds of millions of Christians who have been added to the church in a vast movement that has been under-reported in the West and virtually ignored by the Western elite, including the theological elite. This is the core of the populism I have in mind. It has been chronicled from various angles by Philip Jenkins in books like *The Next Christendom: The Coming of Global Christianity*[9] or *The New Faces of Christianity: Believing the Bible in the Global South*.[10] Mark Noll has also explored these developments in *The New Shape of World Christianity: How American Experience Reflects Global Faith*.[11] Numerous other books could be cited.

How important is this populist presence? Consider that nearly a decade ago Patrick Johnstone in *The Future of the Global Church*[12] wrote of 'the expansion of the mission force in the 20th century'. He stated:

---

8. George Ladd, *A Theology of the New Testament*, rev. ed. (Grand Rapids: Eerdmans, 1993); Donald Guthrie, *New Testament Theology* (Leicester, U.K. and Downers Grove, IL: Inter-Varsity, 1981); I. Howard Marshall, *New Testament Theology* (Downers Grove: IVP Academic, 2014); Frank Thielman, *Theology of the New Testament*, 2nd ed. (Grand Rapids: Zondervan, 2015); Thomas Schreiner, *New Testament Theology* (Grand Rapids: Baker Academic, 2008); Ben Witherington III, *The Indelible Image*, 2 vols. (Downers Grove: InterVarsity, 2009–2010); Craig Blomberg, *A New Testament Theology* (Waco, TX: Baylor University Press, 2018).

9. 3rd ed.; New York: Oxford University Press, 2012.

10. New York: Oxford University Press, 2008.

11. Downers Grove: IVP Academic, 2013.

12. Downers Grove: InterVarsity, 2011, 228.

The mobilization of Christians in missions since 1900 has been astonishing. From 17,400 in 1900, the number rose slowly to 43,000 in 1962, but then came the explosive growth that followed the Awakening around that time, with some 200,000 [missionaries] in 2000 and maybe even 300,000 in 2010. This has happened even as non-evangelical denominational missions collapsed, with the new wave of fervent evangelical missionaries more than replacing them.

Currently the number of missionaries working outside their own countries – increasingly from countries like Brazil, South Korea, Nigeria, and China, not from the West – has been placed at 450,000. It is projected to rise to 550,000 by 2025 and to 700,000 by 2050.[13] There are currently 5,400 foreign mission sending agencies, with 6,000 predicted by 2025 and 7,500 by 2050.[14]

Numbers of Christians in lands receiving and now sending the missionary message have been even more dramatic. Europe *was* Christendom for some 1,000 years. Even in 1900 there were sixty million more Christians in Europe than in Latin America. In 2014, however, Latin America passed Europe as the continent with the most Christians. But only briefly: as of 2018, Africa has passed Latin America. Currently Africa has 599 million Christians and Latin America 597 million. Europe is third, with 550 million. It is reckoned that in 2050 the rankings will be: 1) Africa at 1.25 billion, 2) Latin America at 705 million, 3) Asia at 588 million, and 4) Europe at 490 million. By the way North America is not in the running here: 231 million today, 259 million in 2050.[15]

And in all this we must bear in mind that in lands of recent church growth there are apt to be more Christians who are fervent and Bible-believing, whereas in Europe and North America, many who are booked as Christians socially affirm a faith and practice that is lax, flabby, and culturally compromised by many African, Asian, and Latin American standards.

The rise to prominence of non-Western, Bible-believing Christianity has been taking place as churches led by people trained in elitist New

---

13. For these figures, see Todd M. Johnson, Gina A. Zurlo, Albert W. Hickman, and Peter Crossing, 'Christianity 2019: What's Missing? A Call for Further Research,' *International Bulletin of Missionary Research* 43/1 (January 2019) p. 97.

14. Ibid.

15. For numbers in this paragraph, see Todd M. Johnson, Gina A. Zurlo, Albert W. Hickman, and Peter F. Crossing, 'Christianity 2018: More African Christians and Counting Martyrs,' *International Bulletin of Missionary Research* 42/1 (January 2018) p. 21.

Testament theology have shrunk dramatically. State churches in Europe including the U.K. have long been in precipitous decline. The U.S. experience has been similar. In 1965 denominations in North America associated with the Mainline – many Baptists in the North, the Disciples of Christ, the United Church of Christ, the Episcopalians, and liberal Methodists, Lutherans, and Presbyterians – constituted some 50 per cent of the American population. Today these groups amount to less than 10 per cent of the U.S. population.[16]

Meanwhile, a recent study of Christian leadership in Africa, where over 40 per cent of the world's Protestants are now located, lists this as a major point learned through a massive research project: 'The Bible as the word of God is important in the lives of African Christians.'[17] This is all the more striking as the authority of the Bible, view of the Bible, and importance of the Bible does not seem to have been high on the list of points examined by researchers, who had one question about Bible reading in their hundred question survey instrument.[18] Was this the elite polling the populist? If the Bible is so important, would it not have been helpful to learn much more about how the importance bears itself out, what forms it takes, how it is sustained, where it may go awry, and how it might be enhanced, for starters?

Is there some correlation between continents where skepticism or relative indifference toward the Bible in theological education has been dominant and where churches are collapsing and rates of baptism stagnant or falling? On the surface this is obviously true. And no wonder: elitist reading of Scripture is not designed to foster saving faith *Self-Defeating* in the crucified and risen Jesus but frequently assumes the repugnancy of the gospel diagnosis of the human condition and its remedy. Populist reading, in contrast, which in the West at evangelical institutions engages but declines to affirm the elitist synthesis, and which in much

---

16. Joseph Bottum, *An Anxious Age: The Post-Protestant Ethic and the Spirit of America* (New York: Image, 2014), pp. 88, 90.

17. Robert J. Priest and Kirimi Barine, eds., *African Christian Leadership: Realities, Opportunities, and Impact* (Maryknoll, NY: Orbis, 2017), p. 233.

18. Ibid., pp. 241-78. The single question is on p. 272: How frequently do you read the Bible? Answering 'daily' were these percentages of respondents: in Angola, 60 per cent daily and 27 per cent weekly, in Central African Republic 59 per cent daily and 20 per cent weekly, in Kenya 64 per cent daily and 26 per cent weekly.

of the world knows little of an elitist hermeneutic that denies the truth of the religion it claims to interpret, can be fairly associated with the largest jump in numbers of additions to churches worldwide in history to date.

2. Definitions: Populist and Elitist

2.1 Populist

By populist in this book I mean primarily two things. (1) Populist Christianity refers to the movement whose reading of the Bible (see again my eleven points above) has been under attack by secularist-leaning academicians since at least the seventeenth century. Nicholas Hardy in his book *Criticism and Confession: The Bible in the Seventeenth Century Republic of Letters*[19] has shed new light on the rise of this impulse, represented in that century by Isaac Casaubon, Joseph Justus Scaliger, Hugo Grotius, Louis Cappel, Jean Le Clerc, and Richard Simon. In recent years Ulrich Wilckens (b. 1928) and Klaus Berger (b. 1940) are two well-known New Testament scholars from within the German elite who now very late in their careers have registered protests against their peers. What is this elite vantage point from which populist understanding is critiqued or simply ignored? Thomas Oden has stated it well: 'The point at which modern criticism became ideological advocacy was when it did not allow the ancient writer his own worldview but rather judged that worldview from the viewpoint of an assumed absolutely reliable worldview of scientific forms of knowing spiritual realities.'[20] This is the essence of the elitist position: a hegemonic 'we' of post-biblical times, be it seventeenth century or twenty-first, dismisses the claims of Scripture 'we' find unlikely or unpalatable, and then interprets the Bible in the light of our superior vantage point. A 'populist' reading of Scripture is one that continues to privilege Scripture rather than this superior vantage point.

(2) More positively, populist Christianity as I am defining it refers to groups affirming the view of God, the world, and the church's identity and mission more clearly derivable from the Bible and

---

19. Oxford: Oxford University Press, 2017.

20. Thomas C. Oden, *A Change of Heart: A Personal and Theological Memoir* (Downers Grove: IVP Academic, 2014), p. 166.

representative of historic Christianity. North American seminaries that affirm and uphold statements of faith like the Westminster Confession (Reformed), the Augsburg Confession (Lutheran), or The Baptist Faith and Message (Southern Baptist) are populist as I am defining it. The same essential view is affirmed recently, for example, in the statement 'A Reforming Catholic Confession – What We, Protestants of Diverse Churches and Theological Traditions Say Together.'[21] Its explanatory articles of faith are set forth under these twelve headings: Triune God, Holy Scripture, human beings, fallen-ness, Jesus Christ, the atoning work of Christ, the gospel, the person and work of the Holy Spirit, the church, baptism and the Lord's supper, holy living, and last things. It has been signed by over fourteen hundred leaders from more than sixty countries.

Or one could look at the Lausanne Movement. Its central document set forth in 1974 is called the Lausanne Covenant and begins with these words:

> We, members of the Church of Jesus Christ, from more than 150 nations, participants in the International Congress on World Evangelization at Lausanne, praise God for his great salvation and rejoice in the fellowship he has given us with himself and with each other. We are deeply stirred by what God is doing in our day, moved to penitence by our failures and challenged by the unfinished task of evangelization. We believe the gospel is God's good news for the whole world, and we are determined by his grace to obey Christ's commission to proclaim it to all mankind and to make disciples of every nation. We desire, therefore, to affirm our faith and our resolve, and to make public our covenant.[22]

The early 1970s, when the Lausanne Movement took shape with the encouragement of leading figures like Billy Graham and John Stott, was a period of tumult in increasingly post-Christian societies like the United States. The sexual revolution was hitting its stride. Divorce on demand was becoming the law of the land. Abortion had been legalized. The unraveling of moral fiber whose results are so visible and lamentable today had their origin in this era. Nevertheless, even as ill winds were

---

21. https://reformingcatholicconfession.com/. Accessed January 29, 2019.

22. https://www.lausanne.org/content/covenant/lausanne-covenant. Accessed January 29, 2019.

blowing, seeds of gospel resurgence were being sown at the Lausanne convocation with representatives from more than 150 nations.

In the Lausanne Movement, a high view of Scripture was and continues to be central. The second article of the Lausanne Covenant, after the first article 'The Purpose of God', is entitled 'The Authority and Power of the Bible.' This article states:

> We affirm the divine inspiration, truthfulness and authority of both Old and New Testament Scriptures in their entirety as the only written Word of God, without error in all that it affirms, and the only infallible rule of faith and practice. We also affirm the power of God's Word to accomplish his purpose of salvation. The message of the Bible is addressed to all mankind. For God's revelation in Christ and in Scripture is unchangeable. Through it the Holy Spirit still speaks today. He illumines the minds of God's people in every culture to perceive its truth freshly through their own eyes and thus discloses to the whole church ever more of the many-colored wisdom of God.[23]

Later in the same section stress is laid on the multi-ethnic focus and attraction of Scripture when its message is received so that new life in Christ emerges:

> [The Bible's] inalterability is not a dead, wooden, colorless uniformity. For as the Holy Spirit used the personality and culture of the writers of his Word in order to convey through each something fresh and appropriate, so today *he illumines the minds of God's people in every culture to perceive its truth freshly through their own eyes.* It is he who opens the eyes of our hearts (Eph. 1:17,18), and these eyes and hearts belong to young and old, Latin and Anglo-Saxon, African, Asian and American, male and female, poetic and prosaic. It is this 'magnificent and intricate mosaic of mankind' (to borrow a phrase of Dr Donald McGavran's) which the Holy Spirit uses to disclose from Scripture *ever more of the many-colored wisdom of God* (a literal translation of Eph. 3:10). Thus *the whole church is* needed to receive God's whole revelation in all its beauty and richness (cf. Eph. 3:18 'with all the saints').[24]

In this book, I use 'populist' to refer to the hundreds of millions of Christians worldwide whose understanding and advocacy of the Bible and

---

23. Ibid.

24. https://www.lausanne.org/content/lop/lop-3. Accessed January 29, 2019.

its message comport with such statements. Populists range from illiterate to highly trained – among signatories of 'A Reforming Catholic Confession' are university and seminary presidents and professors, pastors of all stripes, philosophers like Alvin Plantinga, apologists like William Lane Craig, and over fourteen hundred others. But I encountered the same understanding of the Bible and the Christian message among barely literate or illiterate believers over many years of teaching in Sudan. Nor would I say literacy is very high among some North Americans I have encountered in various settings. 'Populist' is therefore well-suited as a descriptive term denoting an outlook common to masses of individuals regardless of their level of learning, geographic location, or economic status. In terms of New Testament theology, populist understanding would generally affirm the readings of the New Testament found in the works mentioned earlier by Guthrie, Marshall, Thielman, Schreiner, Blomberg, and others. But populist understanding would not think it sufficient simply to produce works on New Testament theology for academic consumption. It would see the necessity of personal response to the Bible's saving message and the prioritizing of living out that message and carrying it to those who as yet have resisted it or perhaps have yet to hear.

2.2 Elitist

By elitist I refer to a tradition arising in the wake of the Reformation, but with ideological resemblance to much earlier movements like gnosticism and pagan skeptics like Celsus, who rejected populist reading as described above, which has existed since the first century, and read the Bible in the light of contrasting and often hostile convictions.

Of late several books have been probing the elitist ethos, though not under that label. I have written about it in a *Themelios* article appearing in 2014.[25] At that time I wrote of books by (1) Michael Legaspi, *The Death of Scripture and the Rise of Biblical Studies*,[26] (2) Ulrich Wilckens, *Kritik der Bibelkritik. Wie die Bibel wieder zur Heiligen Schrift werden kann*,[27] and (3) Klaus Berger, *Die Bibelfälscher. Wie wir um die Wahrheit betrogen*

---

25. 'Bye-bye Bible? Progress Report on the Death of Scripture,' *Themelios* 39/3 (November 2014). Accessed at http://themelios.thegospelcoalition.org/article/bye-bye-bible-progress-report-on-the-death-of-scripture on January 26, 2018.

26. Oxford: Oxford University Press, 2011.

27. Neukirchen-Vluyn: Neukirchener Theologie, 2012.

werden.[28] More studies along these lines have emerged since this time, of which I will speak later, but for now we may cite Wilckens for a core characterization of the elitist outlook. It is not new or recent; Nicholas Hardy's book *Criticism and Confession*, describing the then somewhat novel emergence of skeptical readings of Scripture in the seventeenth century, uses 'elite' about a half-dozen times to describe an intellectual cadre of that era who rejected ecclesial interpretation and thereby allegedly furthered knowledge dramatically, because they threw off the shackles of doctrine and biblical authority.[29] Hardy's book challenges this view, and in the course of doing so shows the clay feet and sectarianism of these allegedly more objective and enlightened interpreters.

But to return to Wilckens, he lists five fundamental convictions of scholars going back to the rise of elitist hermeneutics which Hardy places in the seventeenth century. These convictions, he asserts, are still in place for a large segment of those working in biblical studies fields today:

(1) The many miracles in the Bible including those worked by Jesus are at least to be disputed and in most if not all cases denied.

(2) Foremost among the miracles that must be and have been denied is the resurrection of Jesus.

(3) The same unsparing criticism that applies to Christ's resurrection applied to the biblical assertion of the saving power of Christ's death in place of sinners who may be saved by trusting in Him.

(4) Jesus was a moral ethical teacher, the greatest in the history of humankind, whom to follow requires the repudiation of all morals based on authority outside the individual.

(5) The church is no longer necessary for the Christian, and more importantly there is nothing binding about its doctrines for the Christian's faith, nothing normative in its directives for the Christian's life, and nothing authoritative about its leaders for the church's members.

Wilckens published this description of elitist views in 2012. In 2017 he published the final volume of his three-volume New Testament theology.

---

28. München: Pattloch, 2013.

29. Hardy, *Criticism and Confession*, pp. I, 6, 16, 27, 28, 380, 401.

Volume one consists of four separate subvolumes on the history of early Christianity. Volume two consists of two subvolumes tracing the history of various theological themes back to their foundational origin and unity in the reality of God's saving act in the atoning death and the resurrection of Jesus. Volume three, however, extends and expands his book *Kritik der Bibelkritik*. It is called *Historische Kritik der historisch-kritischen Exegese: Von der Aufklärung bis zur Gegenwart.*[30] In translation: *Historical Criticism of Historical-Critical Exegesis: From the Enlightenment to the Present.* As in his earlier book, but in more depth and breadth and with more of a view toward New Testament theology as an academic subfield, Wilckens traces the history of, resistance to, and disastrous effects of reading the Bible with elitist premises. His study culminates in a seven-point proposal under the heading: 'Historical-critical understanding of historical-critical exegesis as presupposition for its theological overhaul.' More on that later. Where ground rules like the ones identified by Wilckens are in effect, overtly or covertly, the result is what I am calling elitist interpretation.

Before I turn to a recent and somewhat dramatic example of it, here is a concise and clear depiction of both populist and elitist understanding from the late nineteenth century. In volume 14 of *Encyclopedia of the Bible and Its Reception*,[31] Friederike Nüssel writes about the systematician and New Testament scholar Martin Kähler (1835–1917). Kähler viewed Schleiermacher's influential theology 'as a virtuous piece of doctrinal art, but without biblical foundation' (col. 1221). To dismiss Schleiermacher marked Kähler as out of step with the burgeoning liberal drift of his day as Albrecht Ritschl and then Adolf Harnack (both following Schleiermacher in important respects) were becoming all the rage. Harnack did not believe in the resurrection, denied the articles of the Apostles' Creed, and called for the church to abandon the Old Testament. Kähler, in contrast, aimed at constructing a *Bibeltheologie* (theology based on the Bible) that acknowledged 'the saving power of biblical witness' existing 'prior to exegetical investigation by means of approved academic methods' (ibid.). For Kähler 'the major task of academic theology is to "track down" this efficacy in the course of

---

30. Göttingen: Vandenhoeck & Ruprecht, 2017.
31. Berlin/Boston: De Gruyter, 2017.

history' (ibid.). Many who had a hand in the Barmen Declaration were students of Kähler, who recognized that 'Christology ... is fundamental to soteriology' and that 'mission is the fundamental task of the church' (col. 1222).

Kähler's approach affirming the truth and power of the Bible's witness prior to academic analysis, and his commitment to academic analysis friendly to confessional understanding rather than dismissive of it, are a distinct example of populist reading in the German university setting, which was rapidly moving in the elitist direction that he was already finding it necessary to defy, along with others of his time like Theodor Zahn (1838–1933), Hermann Cremer (1834–1903), and Adolf Schlatter (1852–1938).

3. Case Study: A Scandinavian Debate

The tension I am highlighting between two approaches to Scripture is ubiquitous in the West today, but generally tacitly and behind the scenes. Sometimes however it leaps forth into the open. This is the case in an exchange found in the *Svensk Exegetisk Årsbok* (Swedish Exegetical Annual), volume 82, 2017.

First there is an article by American New Testament scholar James A. Kelhoffer: 'Simplistic Presentations of Biblical Authority and Christian Origins in the Service of Anti-Catholic Dogma: A Response to Anders Gerdmar.'[32] Kelhoffer previously taught at St Louis University before his current professorship at Uppsala University in Sweden.[33] His article is a twenty-five-page attack on a popular-level book written by another New Testament scholar, a Swede named Anders Gerdmar.[34] Gerdmar

---

32. *Svensk Exegetisk Årsbok* 82 (2017) pp. 154-78. For this and the two other *Svensk Exegetisk Årsbok* essays I refer to in this chapter, I wish to express thanks to Dr Kelhoffer, who kindly sent me offprints. I regret to find that I must differ from him in the positions he has taken in the debate described below.

33. Among Kelhoffer's numerous publications, see *The Diet of John the Baptist: Locusts and Wild Honey in Synoptic and Patristic Interpretation* (2005); *Persecution, Persuasion & Power: Readiness to Withstand Hardship As a Corroboration of Legitimacy in the New Testament* (2010); *Conceptions of 'Gospel' and Legitimacy in Early Christianity* (2014). All three are monographs in the Wissenschaftliche Untersuchungen zum Neuen Testament series published by Mohr Siebeck, Tübingen, Germany.

34. See Anders Gerdmar, *Roots of Theological Anti-Semitism: German Biblical Interpretation and the Jews, from Herder and Semler to Kittel and Bultmann*, Studies in Jewish

responds to Kelhoffer with a twenty-one-page piece entitled 'The End of Innocence: On Religious and Academic Freedom and Intersubjectivity in the Exegetical Craft – A Response to James Kelhoffer.'[35] The exchange concludes with Kelhoffer's reply to Gerdmar entitled 'A Diverse Academy Recognizes No Boundaries for Critical Inquiry and Debate: A Rejoinder to Anders Gerdmar.'[36]

A little background is required to understand this exchange. Gerdmar is not only a scholar but a pastor and preacher. Years ago, he was converted from his liberal Lutheran upbringing to a lively charismatic faith which he still wholeheartedly embraces. A few years ago, a leading charismatic leader in Sweden named Ulf Eckman became Roman Catholic. In the wake of this, Gerdmar was asked by an elderly woman one Sunday, 'Do I need to become a Catholic to be a real Christian?' Gerdmar wrote a pastoral blog response to this question, 'Why I Never Chose to Convert to Roman-Catholicism.' It received so much attention that he expanded it into a 2016 book written in Swedish, the title of which Gerdmar translates as *God's Word Is Enough: Protestant Faith versus Roman-Catholic.*

It is this book that Kelhoffer subjects to withering scrutiny. Below we survey his objections, sketch Gerdmar's response, and finally sample Kelhoffer's rejoinder. The point will be to observe features of the elitist-populist divide that plays out in New Testament theology today.

3.1 A University Objection to a Parish Book

In his highly negative review Kelhoffer notes the impeccable academic credentials of Gerdmar (pp. 154-5).[37] Gerdmar has authored two major monographs in New Testament studies (see Works Cited at the end of this book) and with Kari Syreeni is co-author of a widely-used Swedish textbook on academic study of the New Testament.[38] Gerdmar belongs

---

History and Culture 20 (Leiden/Boston: Brill, 2010); *Rethinking the Judaism-Hellenism Dichotomy: A Historiographical Case Study of 2 Peter and Jude*, Coniectanea Biblica, New Testament Series 36 (Stockholm: Almqvist & Wiksell, 2001).

35. *Svensk Exegetisk Årsbok* 82 (2017) pp. 179-209.

36. Ibid., pp. 210-22.

37. Page numbers in this section refer to Kelhoffer's 'Simplistic Presentations of Biblical Authority and Christian Origins in the Service of Anti-Catholic Dogma: A Response to Anders Gerdmar' referred to above.

38. Anders Gerdmar with Kari Syreeni, *Vägar till Nya Testamentet. Tekniker, metoder och verktyg för nytestamentlig exegetik* (Lund: Studentlitteratur, 2006).

to the Society of New Testament Studies and to other learned societies. He is also an associate professor at Uppsala University.[39] Nevertheless, his book affirming Protestant belief rather than Roman Catholic draws fire from Kelhoffer on numerous accounts, only six of which we can allude to here. But this will be enough to verify what 'elitism' as we are defining it looks like.

First, Gerdmar's book affirms pre-critical views that Kelhoffer argues scholars have abandoned. Since Gerdmar 'presents his arguments as though they were based on sound scholarship and legitimized by his own academic standing', someone like Kelhoffer needs to challenge Gerdmar. Otherwise, the 'uncritical views' he espouses may 'foster the construction of a parallel moral and religious universe, from whose vantage point' people like Gerdmar 'can lament and assail the results of nonconfessional' scholarship (pp. 155-6). We may already note here Kelhoffer's apparent assumption that there is no other moral and religious vantage point than the one he takes his department at Uppsala University to represent, at least not one from which the elite view could be called in question.[40] Moreover, it is wrong to 'lament and assail' this academic vantage point on the basis of views that Uppsala does not endorse. The elitist academy is and should be unassailable, even by someone like Gerdmar who has academic credentials.

Second, Kelhoffer objects that Gerdmar misrepresents how important 'faith in all of God's Word' is as 'the primary basis of the common Christian faith' (p. 159). Gerdmar asserts that Catholics add to the Bible by authoritative ecclesial tradition and liberals cancel parts out, both charges which are too often true, in my opinion. But Kelhoffer thinks that critical discovery of the Bible's irreducible internal diversity, not unity, proves Gerdmar wrong (see also p. 169 on the New Testament's *teachings*, plural, not *teaching*, singular, on sin and grace; for Kelhoffer the sources' affirmations on these subjects are disparate and evidently irreconcilable). Kelfhoffer appeals to James Barr's book

---

39. http://www.andersgerdmar.com/curriculum-vitae/. Accessed January 29, 2019.

40. Kelhoffer protests later in the debate that he is not implying the existence of only two possible universes and that Gerdmar misinterprets him at that point. But I understood him the way Gerdmar did in my first reading of Kelhoffer's review and believe it is a fair depiction of his position, which is clearly binary (either/or) when it comes to his view versus Gerdmar's.

Fundamentalism from forty years ago and a slightly more recent article by Nancy Ammerman (about twenty-five years ago) in support (p. 159 n. 19), as if Barr and Ammerman prove that viewing the Bible as the source of Christian unity is bogus. Kelhoffer adds that 'biblical literature says precious little about faith in the written word' and that 'Jesus' teachings stress the centrality of faith in God' (pp. 159-60), statements that the works of just a single New Testament scholar of another era thoroughly refute: B. B. Warfield, whose heritage in finding a high view of the Bible affirmed by the Bible and by Jesus continues in numerous recent works on the Bible's full truthfulness.[41] Moreover, it should be pointed out that if Scripture is God-given (*theopneustos*; 2 Tim. 3:16) personal communication, there is not a great distance between 'faith in the written word' and 'faith in God'. Just as to trust in Kelhoffer's words (or not) is to trust in Kelhoffer and not Gerdmar, to have faith in Scripture can be tantamount to having faith in God and not alternatives.

In addition, Kelhoffer's avowal that the Bible says little about faith in the written Word is wildly out of sympathy with the practice of Jesus in the Gospels, the testimony of Acts, and the usage of most other New Testament writings in their frequent reference to and dependence on Old Testament Scripture. From well back into the first century we have evidence of early church dependence on New Testament scripture as well, as not only in 1 Timothy 5:18 (referring to Luke 10:7) and 2 Peter 3:15 (referring to Paul's writings), but also in the writings of figures nearly contemporary with the apostles like Clement of Rome, Papias, Polycarp, and Ignatius.

Nor does Kelhoffer refer to extensive scholarship by John Woodbridge which shows that, indeed, the historic position of the church has been

---

41. On Warfield see, e.g., Fred G. Zaspel, *The Theology of B. B. Warfield: A Systematic Summary* (Wheaton: Crossway, 2010). For his writings on the Bible including Jesus' heavy recourse to the written word, see *The Works of Benjamin B. Warfield*, 10 vols. (New York: Oxford University Press, 1932), esp. vols. 1 (*Revelation and Inspiration*), 2 (*Biblical Doctrines*), 3 (*Christology and Criticism*), and 10 (*Critical Reviews*). For just three of a dozen or more substantial recent accounts of Scripture's truth and authority (many aiming in part to commemorate the Protestant Reformation), see Peter A. Lillback and Richard B. Gaffin, Jr., *Thy Word Is Still Truth: Essential Writings on the Doctrine of Scripture from the Reformation to Today* (Phillipsburg, PA: P&R, 2013); D. A. Carson, ed., *The Enduring Authority of the Christian Scriptures* (Grand Rapids/Cambridge, U.K.: Eerdmans, 2016); and Craig Blomberg, *The Historical Reliability of the New Testament: Countering Challenges to Evangelical Christian Beliefs* (Nashville: B&H Academic, 2016).

that all of Scripture is inspired by God and true in what it asserts, rightly interpreted.[42] Biblical inerrancy, Woodbridge has repeatedly shown, has always been a point of at least Western Christian unity, and a point on which Catholics and Protestants at the Reformation agreed, apart from Rome's insistence that their church teachings trumped Scripture when they come in conflict, the key disagreement giving rise to the Reformation. So again in this case, Kelhoffer's objection is based on the elitist position that (1) there never was a 'faith in all of God's Word' because the academy has shown that Scripture is diverse and internally self-contradictory from the start, and (2) literature demonstrating the contrary is irrelevant since it does not agree with what their scholarship affirms.

Along these same lines Kelhoffer objects to Gerdmar's assertion that an 'uncomplicated hermeneutic' permits recognition of the truth of God's Word (pp. 160-1). This is, of course, an application of the principle of the perspicuity of Scripture, which says that the saving message of the Bible is accessible to any seeking reader. But Kelhoffer points to Gerdmar's academic textbook which explains hermeneutics in far more nuanced terms. He does not seem to consider that Gerdmar could be speaking first of reading the Bible in and for saving faith, and then reading it within the ground rules prevailing in an academic setting, where things are more complicated, as Gerdmar well knows.

Third, at every turn Kelhoffer insists on enforcing what he takes to be the consensus of critical opinion as the law to which Gerdmar is subject. Gerdmar thinks he is writing a pastoral book commending Protestant faith; because he ignores critical discussion and challenges Catholic belief (as if Catholic belief does not daily around the world challenge Protestant faith), Kelhoffer attributes to his book a 'polemical agenda'. Gerdmar does not inform his readers that 'most biblical scholars' opted for non-Pauline authorship of Colossians and Ephesians 'decades ago', according to Kelhoffer; what Gerdmar should have done in his book, when disagreeing with the critical consensus, is (1) 'acknowledge the

---

42. See, e.g., John D. Woodbridge, *Biblical Authority: A Critique of the Rogers/McKim Proposal* (Grand Rapids: Zondervan, 1982); idem, 'Evangelical Self-Identity and the Doctrine of Biblical Inerrancy,' in Andreas Köstenberger and Robert Yarbrough, eds., *Understanding the Times* (Wheaton: Crossway, 2010), pp. 104-38. More recently see Woodbridge, 'Sola Scriptura: Original Intent, Historical Development and Import for Christian Living,' *Presbyterion* 44/1 (Spring 2018) pp. 4-24.

existence of dissension among learned colleagues,' and (2) argue for his own position (p. 163). But given Kelhoffer's faith in the critical consensus, it is hard to imagine what arguments Gerdmar could have advanced in a popular-level book commending the saving gospel message that Kelhoffer would deem convincing.

Three other areas, more briefly, where Gerdmar transgresses because Kelhoffer asserts that scholars prove him wrong: (1) The 'early recognition of a NT canon of Scripture' (p. 162). (2) Gerdmar is out of step with the 'scholarly consensus' on Marcion and the gnostics, and he gives uncritical caricatures of Irenaeus and other patristic figures (p. 164). (3) Gerdmar assumes as apostolic not only Ephesians and Colossians, which are not from Paul, but 1-2 Thessalonians, 1-2 Timothy, and Titus, which are not from Paul either (p. 165). Kelhoffer states, '1 Peter and 2 Peter apparently stem from two different pseudonymous authors and have no direct connection to the historical apostle Peter' (p. 165). He appeals for support to well-known names in what I am calling the elitist tradition: Helmut Koester, John H. Elliott, Udo Schnelle, Bart Ehrman. He does not acknowledge any of the many scholars who have argued plausibly against the elitist consensus.

Kelhoffer registers a number of other objections. One that must have felt particularly galling was Kelhoffer's patronizing speculation on how 'in the decades subsequent to G.[erdmar]'s crisis as a young theology student, he might have developed as a scholar and a person of faith if he had found adequate guidance from the remedies offered in [James] Barr's *Beyond Fundamentalism*' (p. 177). Having implied that Gerdmar is psychologically impaired, Kelhoffer then draws for support on a 1984 article by David Parker which casts fundamentalism as a cult, seemingly relegating Gerdmar's convictions to that sinister, benighted status.

In any case, Kelhoffer concludes, 'The academy [note there is only one, and it trumps everything that even an academically qualified Christian pastor might say in urging saving faith from the Bible as he sees it at a parishioner's request] has a responsibility to speak out when its credentials are being co-opted to legitimize the dissemination of such misinformation' (p. 178). Kelhoffer has rendered the elite verdict.

Is there any way at all for Gerdmar to utter a peep in self-defense at such a scathing attack?

3.2 A Populist Response to Elitist Scruples[43]

Gerdmar's response is summarized both at the beginning and end of his article entitled 'The End of Innocence: On Religious and Academic Freedom and Intersubjectivity in the Exegetical Craft – A Response to James Kelhoffer.' At the beginning he lists these points (pp. 179-80): (1) Why did an academic journal publish in English 'a review of a confessional and popular book' written in Swedish, so that readers can only evaluate Kelhoffer's claims against the book if they can read Swedish? (2) Kelhoffer applies academic rules to a work of pastoral and confessional instruction, and in doing so 'takes on a role that is confessional rather than scholarly.' (3) Gerdmar thinks the academy should be open to many viewpoints, 'whereas Kelhoffer seems to favour that one consensus should rule.' (4) Kelhoffer asserts but does not show that Gerdmar's views on scholarly matters have no scholarly justification. (5) Kelhoffer, by his 'baseless speculations about [Gerdmar] and Christian leaders who … endorsed the book, … erects a wall between his department at Uppsala University and large portions of Swedish Christianity.'

Particulars of Gerdmar's defense of his book and of his hermeneutical understanding and practice are thorough in this article and cannot be detailed here. But one part of his response underscores a central aspect of the populist-elitist divide we are examining.

Kelhoffer charges that Gerdmar's counsel to rely on God's Word alone will lead to an 'overconfidence among those convinced that they possess a, or the, correct understanding of the Bible, as confirmed by their ecstatic experiences' (p. 202). Gerdmar replies that he does not make that argument in his book but rather states to the contrary that 'every kind of prophecy and similar charismatic phenomena is [sic] subordinated to the written Word of God.' Moreover, he accuses Kelhoffer of uninformed prejudice against what missiologists call the fourth church tradition (i.e., the Charismatics, along with Roman Catholic, Orthodox, and Protestant). And Gerdmar points out that there are 250,000 charismatics in Sweden with numbers growing, with only 305,000 free-church and evangelical Lutherans in that country with

---

43. Page numbers in this section refer to Gerdmar's 'The End of Innocence: On Religious and Academic Freedom and Intersubjectivity in the Exegetical Craft – A Response to James Kelhoffer' noted above.

their numbers declining. Gerdmar concludes: 'Informing this growing movement in the areas of exegesis and hermeneutics is an important task, whereas Kelhoffer without substantiation expresses his prejudice about this "fourth tradition" of Christianity' (p. 203).

It is fair to say that Gerdmar gives a reasonable account of his book, his outlook, and his understanding that there are conventions for academic interchange, on the one hand, and for confessional understanding and practice on the other. He states he does not think it is the business of anyone at Uppsala University what Gerdmar, or a Roman Catholic, or anyone else 'does in church', or if they attend no church at all. He ironically quotes words from Kelhoffer's own installation lecture at Uppsala (p. 209): 'A university shall not allow discrimination based on religious confession or other factors. Opportunities to study and conduct research in theology and religious studies shall be open not just to liberal Lutherans, Catholics, and agnostics but, indeed, to all who value critical examination and scholarly methods of inquiry.' Nevertheless, as we will see shortly, Kelhoffer is adamant that Gerdmar has betrayed elite protocol and gone over to the dark side of pre-critical conviction.

I am reminded of a book published over twenty years ago by Daniel Patte, then chair of religious studies at Vanderbilt University. The book was called *Ethics of Biblical Interpretation*.[44] Patte argued for the legitimacy of *every* hermeneutical vantage point in interpreting the Bible – whether 'feminist, womanist, mujerista, African-American, Hispanic-American, Native-American, and/or third-world liberation theologians and biblical scholars' (p. 115). He called such non- or quasi-academic readings from outside the guild 'ordinary' readings and bade them all welcome, for in a sense even guild readings are 'ordinary' too. All readings deserve a place at the table. There was just one exception: 'evangelical fundamentalists' whose 'appeal to the authority of the text is a smoke screen hiding a betrayal of the text' (p. 80). Interpreters of biblical texts can legitimately belong to any hermeneutical orientation they wish except for one. Ironically, the forbidden orientation comports with the view of Scripture and its message that is dominant (outside of elitist strongholds) around the world.

44. Louisville: Westminster/John Knox, 1995. See my review in *JETS* 40/1 (March 1997) pp. 128-9.

3.3 A Tom Petty Ending[45]

What is Kelhoffer's response to Gerdmar's defense? Basically this: 'I won't back down.'[46] I don't think Kelhoffer concedes a single point of correction or qualification to his original attack.

But I believe it is possible to summarize a key consideration in their disagreement. Gerdmar says we are dealing with a clash of two defensible viewpoints. He defends his confessional and pastoral presentation of biblical evidence for the sake of presenting the Protestant understanding of the Bible's gospel message in contrast to Catholic teaching. He does not deny Kelhoffer his historical-critical vantage point. He is a publishing participant in the academic himself. He does deny that Kelhoffer's vantage point itself is free from its own dogmatic assumptions. Operating within his competency and calling as both a scholar and a pastor, Gerdmar thinks his book, its factual claims, and its expository and evangelistic aims, in addition to being consistent with historic confessional conviction, are also not a betrayal of academic integrity.

While Kelhoffer says he is open to multiple perspectives, he echoes Patte above in denying Gerdmar his perspective. And here is the reason as stated in his interchange with Gerdmar: Kelhoffer regards as unassailable 'the gains of 200 years of historical criticism' (p. 216). While Kelhoffer denies that he holds 'an extreme hierarchical and positivist position' (p. 217), it probably sounds like he does to Gerdmar when Kelhoffer appeals to the last 200 years of historical criticism, which *has* undeniably been 'hierarchical and positivist', or when Kelhoffer writes:

> There are certain views that fall outside the diverse chorus of scholarly voices that fervently engage in academic debates. No amount of listening to other voices is going to increase the likelihood that the apostle Paul would, as [Gerdmar assumes in his book], have written a letter like Ephesians (p. 217).

Kelhoffer also rejects as even discussible the possibility that the New Testament writings were received as Scripture in the first century. He also rejects as even discussible the possibility of a unified, not diverse, message from the New Testament documents.

---

45. Page numbers refer to Kelhoffer's 'A Diverse Academy Recognizes No Boundaries for Critical Inquiry and Debate: A Rejoinder to Anders Gerdmar' noted above.

46. Those words were the title of a song released in April 1989 as the lead single from Tom Petty's first solo album, *Full Moon Fever*.

In conclusion, we are dealing with an elitist reading of the New Testament and its message. Kelhoffer claims that he is 'neither confessional nor anti-confessional' when charging that Gerdmar's book is a breach of scholarship (p. 214). Kelhoffer, we could say, sees certain truths of criticism as revelatory in status, the elitist guild consensus functioning like the papal magisterium. Against these truths no warranted objections are possible. Gerdmar regards Scripture as revelatory, as empirically plausible despite the attacks mounted against it by 'critical' Western scholarship over the past few centuries, and as valid as written for 'teaching, for reproof, for correction, for training in righteousness' (2 Tim. 3:16 NASB), not because he is a fideist or psychologically stunted or unethical, as Kelhoffer implies, but because he thinks the texts he interprets, the historic Christian faith that informs his reading, and arguable historical evidence all justify his reading. He also touches on the hermeneutical relevance of masses of Swedish charismatic Bible believers who resonate with his interpretive approach, as pointed out above.

We have, now, presented what this chapter title promised: a depiction of 'the enduring "critical" objection to "confessional" reading of Scripture,' using the less familiar descriptors 'populist' and 'elitist'. This objection is several hundred years old and persists today. Our next chapter will trace where this faceoff is taking New Testament theology in at least some influential quarters.

CHAPTER TWO

The Enduring Appeal of Neo-Allegorical Interpretation: Baur and Bultmann Redux

1. Introduction: Review and Clarification

The previous chapter took up 'the enduring "critical" objection to "confessional" reading of Scripture'. But I did not follow standard histories like those by Stephen Neill and Tom Wright,[1] or Werner Georg Kümmel,[2] or William Baird.[3] Instead, I took a back door route, avoiding what Stephen D. Moore and Yvonne Sherwood in their book *The Invention of the Biblical Scholar* call 'a traditional history of historical-critical scholarship'.[4] They gently mock such a history as 'an aetiological saga in which the authentically "historical" and "critical" identity markers arrive in increments until the features in the emerging portrait have been transformed into our own.'[5] Rather than speak of 'historical-critical' or 'critical', I employed the term elitist, offset in the previous chapter by their counterparts I called 'populist'.

---

1. Stephen Neill and Tom Wright, *The Interpretation of the New Testament 1861–1986*, 2nd ed. (Oxford: Oxford University Press, 1988).

2. W. G. Kümmel, *The New Testament: The History of the Investigation of its Problems* (Nashville: Abingdon, 1972).

3. William Baird, *History of New Testament Research*, volume 1: *From Deism to Tübingen*; volume two: *From Jonathan Edwards to Rudolf Bultmann*; volume 3: *From C. H. Dodd to H. D. Betz* (Minneapolis: Fortress, 1992–2013).

4. Stephen D. Moore and Yvonne Sherwood, *The Invention of the Biblical Scholar: A Critical Manifesto* (Minneapolis: Fortress, 2011), x.

5. Ibid.

I will grant that 'elitist' could be felt as polemical by those identifying with its convictions, just as 'populist' could be felt as insulting. I intend neither pejorative insinuation. I intend it as frankly descriptive, and even a little sympathetic to each view in how it views the other. Yet a few additional clarifying remarks are in order.

1.1 'Elitist' Clarified

Elitists will surely admit that their official guild interest in the Bible has little in common with the hundreds of millions of believers, many charismatic, who have poured into churches in recent generations affirming the Bible and its foundational teachings in general conformity with what Thomas Oden has called 'classic consensual Christianity'.[6] James Kelhoffer's pique at Anders Gerdmar (previous chapter) exemplifies the elite academy's aversion to seeing the pure water of its findings and convictions mixed with the tainted oil of evangelistic and charismatic Christianity. It is standard in the histories that 'critical' study of the Bible arises with the enlightened rejection of Christian doctrinal interpretation of it. So what is interpretation of the Bible about from the elitist vantage point? That question has many answers. But a central answer is found in Moore and Sherwood, *Invention of the Biblical Scholar*. Here is their description of 'biblical scholarship in the twenty-first century': it is

> a critical subgenre that had tended overwhelmingly to think in terms of the discipline's continued survival and self-sustenance through continued methodological innovation, and that typically translates into advocacy for those new methods that seem to sit most solidly and securely upon the foundations established by the older methods.[7]

Historic Christian, or what I am calling, with an eye to the world's teeming masses of new and poor Christians, 'populist' interpreters, have a very different regard for the Bible. They seek to understand, appropriate, benefit from, spread, and where needed defend the Bible's message, not reinterpret that message on the basis of an endless progression of self-referential methods based on skepticism toward it.

---

6. Thomas C. Oden, *A Change of Heart: A Personal and Theological Memoir* (Downers Grove: IVP Academic, 2014), e.g., pp. 148, 150, 161 (combined with 'paleo-orthodoxy'), pp. 196, 304, 334.

7. Moore and Sherwood, *Invention of the Biblical Scholar*, p. 131.

At this time, the elitist response to populist regard for Scripture in its manifold international manifestations seems most commonly to be obliviousness. Biblical scholarship is about developing new methods based on the old ones, not about adjusting in the light of the living christological truth that populist Christianity across continents and cultures purports to derive from the Bible. Populists think Jesus is Lord, risen from the grave and interceding at God's right hand, from whence He will return to judge the living and the dead, and that biblical interpretation should factor that in, since Scripture was given by the Spirit who proceeds from the Father and the Son. Elite interpreters seem most often to deny the relevance of such conviction in the academic setting and either tacitly or overtly suppress the incursion of such embarrassing claims, even though they are glaringly prominent in the New Testament documents. Given the high level of academic training of 'critical' scholars, their social locations in world universities and seminaries, the commercial and financial and political and media support they enjoy, and their commitment not to interpret the Bible with sympathy for its meaning as populist Christianity understands it, the descriptive term 'elitist' is fitting.

1.2 'Populist' Clarified

A clarifying and critical word regarding 'populist' is in order as well. At its worst, 'populism' could refer to manifestations of Christianity that are ignorant, conservative in culpable ways, anti-intellectual, manipulative, and immoral through complicity in sins like racism, nationalism, and materialism. That is a very short list.

Let me elaborate briefly with reference just to the United States. Much of the U.S. evangelical population, as I see it, is deeply compromised by factors that stand in tension with biblical and Christian principles and commitments. U.S. evangelicalism (which with its generally high view of Scripture has close ties at least formally to populist Christian faith on other continents) is as much in need of renewal from new Christian impulses on other continents as elitism is. Nathan Hatch's study *The Democratization of American Christianity* remains a valuable look at a past whose legacy still defines the evangelical present in too many ways.[8] These ways include, to name just five broad areas:

---

8. Nathan O. Hatch, *The Democratization of American Christianity* (New Haven and London: Yale University Press, 1989).

(1) disinterest in, bordering on hostility toward, historic theological systems and 'theology' in general;

(2) anti-clericalism rendering a minister's direction and care of souls unwelcome if not distasteful;

(3) a mis-shapen doctrine of the priesthood of the believer that mitigates against biblical and ecclesial authority and encourages a prideful religious solipsism;

(4) increasing biblical illiteracy, especially of the Old Testament, coupled with an ethical indifference that combine to make violation of biblical commands and teachings increasingly routine even within the church; and

(5) transmutation of the call to Jesus' cross into an enablement system in support of enjoying diverse permutations of some secularist dream (e.g., life, liberty, and the pursuit of happiness, all of these things defined by the *polis* and not by the *ecclesia*). In the U.S. the *ecclesia* too often becomes an extension of the *polis* – this is indicated in the current overlap of political and religious ideals in both left-wing and right-wing circles.

But not all the U.S. evangelical population has bowed to Baal, and anyway, as of 2018, about 41 per cent of Protestants in the world are in Africa. By 2050, 53.1 per cent of Protestants in the world will be in Africa.[9] This does not count African Protestants on other continents. By comparison, today just 16 per cent of Protestants in the world are found in Europe, and only 11 per cent in North America. Asia has more than either at this time: 18 per cent. By 2050, Europe will have just 10 per cent of the world's Protestants, North America will shrink to 8 per cent, and Asia will hold about steady at 17 per cent.[10] American evangelical decadence does not automatically taint the 89 per cent of Protestants in the world who reside elsewhere.

1.3 'Populist' and Its Challenge

In this book I define populist not primarily with reference to decadent American evangelicalism, which exists and may be declining in

---

9. Figures are from Todd M. Johnson, Gina A. Zurlo, Albert W. Hickman, and Peter Crossing, 'Christianity 2017: Five Hundred Years of Protestant Christianity,' *International Bulletin of Missionary Research* 41/1 (January 2017) pp. 41-52.

10. Ibid.

numbers and worsening in character, but to the 70 per cent or higher percentage of the world's Protestants who are in Latin America, Africa, and Asia, and who largely affirm the Bible's historical and doctrinal truth. I am, in a word, pressing the late Lamin Sanneh's question, lodged, as he admits, from 'the margin',[11] in that he is an African Muslim convert and not a theologian or biblical scholar proper. He criticizes mainstream Western theology as 'a domesticated activity of the mind'.[12] He says 'standard exegesis spins faith into just more cultural filibuster'.[13] It is hard not to think of Paul's mention of those who are 'always learning and never able to arrive at a knowledge of the truth' (2 Tim. 3:7 NASB). Sanneh asks how Western elites (my term not his; he speaks of 'Europeans') 'can continue ... to study and teach Christianity without paying heed to examples of Christianity's successful cross-border expansion in postcolonial societies.'[14] Of course he knew the answer: just look around.

Sanneh regarded Christianity not just in Oden's sense as an historic integrated entity but also as a dramatically renewing one that is transforming continents before our eyes, yet is being stonewalled by the theological and exegetical elite. Sanneh states: 'Christianity is a world religion of recent vintage with energy to renew the church as it reels exhausted from its pact with secularism.' A pact with secularism! Reeling exhausted, like a prize fighter back-peddling toward the ropes! I can't think of a better description of the current plight of elitism which for over two hundred years has forsaken a theological orientation in favor of a liberal idealist vantage point steered most of all by an oligarchy of key post-Christian German thinkers like Kant, Hegel, Schelling and Schleiermacher.[15] In North America we often hear additional key names thrown in – Marx, Freud, Nietzsche, Heidegger – and not just Germans: we add in French theorists like Derrida and Foucault. While societies

---

11. See his autobiographical reflection *Summoned from the Margin: Homecoming of an African* (Grand Rapids/Cambridge, U.K.: Eerdmans, 2012).

12. Lamin Sanneh, *Whose Religion Is Christianity? The Gospel beyond the West* (Grand Rapids/Cambridge, U.K.: Eerdmans, 2003), p. 57f.

13. Ibid., p. 59.

14. Ibid., p. 58.

15. Gary Dorrien. *Kantian Reason and Hegelian Spirit: The Idealistic Logic of Modern Theology* (Chichester, West Sussex, U.K.: Wiley-Blackwell, 2012).

with church ministers trained in Western elite thought have largely dismantled their once-great state churches (in Europe) and mainline ones (in North America), swarms of subgroups preaching Jesus from the Bible have, as Sanneh indicates, electrified the world religions scene, often from the social and economic bottom up.

Contrary to the secularization hypothesis, which posits that as the world becomes more technologically advanced it will become less religious, the opposite is occurring. As Martin Marty has remarked, 'anyone with a global vision will find evidence that' the secularization hypothesis 'was off the mark in a world in which *both* "the secular" *and* "the religious" increase in power. It is not a "religionless world" and is not becoming one.'[16] Marty rightly identifies the tension in outlook to which this book calls attention. Something dramatic has taken place, expressed in this recent book title: *The Unexpected Christian Century: The Reversal and Transformation of Global Christianity, 1900–2000.*[17]

2. A Significant Present Development: Return to Baur and Bultmann

If my hunch is justified that elitist interpretation of the New Testament, epitomized in the New Testament theology arising since F. C. Baur (and before), and culminating in Bultmann, merits fresh assessment in light of a populist surge in world Christianity, today's renewed interest in both these long-dead figures is surprising and somewhat ominous. Let us consider Baur first.

2.1 New Interest in F. C. Baur (1792–1860)

Perhaps the classic English-language history of New Testament interpretation, with notable emphasis on its theological interpretation and in that sense New Testament theology, is Stephen Neill's brilliant *The Interpretation of the New Testament 1861–1961*, which with Tom Wright's help was later updated through 1986.[18] Few passages of that great book are more stirring, or more patent of ridicule if you are

---

16. Martin Marty, *Dietrich Bonhoeffer's* Letters and Papers from Prison: *A Biography* (Princeton and Oxford: Princeton University Press, 2011), p. 239 (my italics).

17. Authored by Scott W. Sundquist (Grand Rapids: Baker Academic, 2015).

18. Oxford: Oxford University Press, 1988

elitist, than the one depicting the rise of F. C. Baur and the Tübingen school[19]:

> For it must be recognized that the threat presented to the Christian cause by the school of Tübingen was very grave. It is, of course, a fact that no one is saved merely by believing that certain events happened a long time ago. But it is a long way from this naïve belief to the bland assertion that the idea is all that matters, that the historical self-clothing of the idea would remain even if it could be proved that none of these historical events, which have been regarded as the foundation of the Christian faith, had ever occurred at all. If the incarnation of Jesus Christ is the great act of God in history, then much does depend on the extent and reliability of our historical evidence for what happened.[20]

In Neill's very English telling, Victorian Christianity in the 1860s fell into panic at the German threat. But not to fear: from an English quarter arose deliverance.

> A way out of the panic could be found only if men would come forward who would carry out the work of critical investigation in a spirit of complete fearlessness, with willingness to face every fact and every issue, to meet them less hampered by presuppositions than the representatives of the German schools, and to show on the basis of minutely critical work that the answers given to the critical questions in Germany between 1830 and 1860 were not the only answers that were compatible with the known facts. The hour brought forth the man; in 1861 Joseph Barber Lightfoot was appointed to the Hulsean Professorship of Divinity at Cambridge, being then thirty-three years of age.[21]

No less dramatic is Neill's account of how Lightfoot's scholarship, supported by the equally decisive findings of German scholar Theodor Zahn and the confirmation of Adolf Harnack, dealt a death blow to Baur's theories. Among these theories were claims that (1) much of

---

19. An intellectual movement centered at the University of Tübingen ca. 1835–1860 and associated first of all with Baur. Baur interpreted the New Testament based on a panentheistic doctrine of God. In his reading, the New Testament points to a philosophical ideal, not God's incarnate self-disclosure through Christ in accordance with Scripture (cf. Rom. 1:2; 16:26). A core historical dynamic for the unfolding of this ideal was interpersonal strife among early Christian groups. A Jewish (Petrine) party emphasizing Jesus' messianic awareness was opposed by a Gentile (Pauline) party focusing on Jesus' ethical idealism and universalism.

20. Neill, *The Interpretation of the New Testament 1861–1961*, p. 34.

21. Ibid.

the New Testament was written in the middle of the second century or later; (2) Christ's resurrection was never a real historical event but merely a mental impression that occurred to Saul of Tarsus; and (3) we have no access to the historical setting of Jesus' teachings in the Gospel writings; we possess only the reflex of unknown writers' subjectivity. I would add that Baur's hypothesis that Jew-Gentile partisanship, in the form of a Petrine-Pauline antagonism, is the fundamental historical dynamic explaining the rise of the Christian movement, has proven to be simplistic and equally untenable.

So slender-to-nonexistent is the real 'historical' basis for Baur's view of New Testament history, in fact, that I would argue that his entire reconstruction qualifies to be viewed as allegory. I am expanding here on Richard Bauckham's observation regarding Gospels criticism in its stress since the 1960s on how 'each Gospel addresses the specific situation of a particular Christian community'.[22] This has led, he asserts, to 'the development of more or less allegorical readings of the gospel' based on various imaginatively conceived communities resulting in what 'looks like a kind of historical fantasy'.[23]

In Bauckham's words, 'The principle that the Gospels inform us not about Jesus but about the church is taken so literally that the narrative, ostensibly about Jesus, has to be understood as an allegory in which the community tells its own story.'[24] Klyne Snodgrass has recently argued in a similar vein against J. P. Meier. In Meier's magisterial five volumes entitled *A Marginal Jew: Rethinking the Historical Jesus*, Meier argues that only four parables out of the nearly four dozen found in the New Testament can be traced back to Jesus. Most are early church creations. Snodgrass rightly responds that the early church did not tell parables.[25] If Snodgrass is right, Meier's method, like Baur's, results in a historiography that bears comparison with allegory.

Just as Gospels criticism at times goes off the rails by foregrounding an imagined and unverifiable historical setting that cuts against the grain

Allegorical [Explained]

---

22. *The Gospel for All Christians* (Grand Rapids: Eerdmans, 1998), p. 19.

23. Ibid., p. 20.

24. Ibid.

25. Klyne Snodgrass, 'Are the Parables Still the Bedrock of the Jesus Tradition?' *Journal of the Study of the Historical Jesus* 15/1 (2017), pp. 131-46.

of the Gospels' own historical claims, so Baur based his anti-theological interpretation of the New Testament on any number of hypotheses that did not find wide acceptance to start with and that over time have repeatedly proven to have meager empirical justification. For that reason, in this chapter I have called his approach, as I will Bultmann's, neo-allegorical.

So why are we even talking about F. C. Baur in 2018? Neill helps us here; he observes, 'One of the curious features in German theology is that no ghost is ever laid [to rest]. A century after his death Baur still walks abroad, and echoes of his ideas are found in all kinds of places.'[26]

That statement from 1964[27] is turning out to be true today. The year 2014 saw the appearance of a major anthology of fifteen essays on Baur under the title *Ferdinand Christian Baur and the History of Early Christianity*.[28] A figure of his stature and effect deserves revisiting every few generations. More surprising, however, is the publication in 2016 of Baur's crowning life work, *Lectures on New Testament Theology*.[29] This had been preceded in 2014 by Baur's *History of Christian Dogma*.[30] Longtime Baur supporter Robert Morgan of Linacre College at Oxford offers this on the dust jacket of Baur's New Testament theology: 'this great synthesis should correct some stale stereotypes and give due recognition to a genius unjustly neglected outside Germany. It could also contribute to the revival of critical New Testament theology.'

Comments are in order on this anthology of essays on Baur. We will not explore particulars of Baur's *Lectures on New Testament Theology*, with which I have dealt elsewhere in some detail.[31]

2.2 Exploration of Current Baur Scholarship

The book *Ferdinand Christian Baur and the History of Early Christianity* testifies to the intellectual sophistication of Baur's publications, to the

---

26. Neill and Wright, *Interpretation of the New Testament 1861-1986*, p. 62.

27. The year the first edition of *Interpretation of the New Testament 1861–1961* appeared.

28. Martin Bauspiess, Christof Landmesser, and David Lincicum, eds., *Ferdinand Christian Baur und die Geschichte des frühen Christentums*, Wissenschaftliche Untersuchungen zum Neuen Testament 333 (Tübingen: Mohr Siebeck, 2014).

29. Ed. Peter C. Hodgson, trans. Robert F. Brown (Oxford: University Press, 2016). The German edition appeared in 1864.

30. Ed. Peter C. Hodgson, trans. Robert F. Brown and Peter C. Hodgson (Oxford: University Press, 2016). The German edition appeared in 1858.

31. See my *The Salvation Historical Fallacy?* (Leiden: Deo, 2004).

prodigious scope of his output, and to the suggestiveness of many of his strategies as he wrote extensively in the areas of New Testament introduction and exegesis, early church history and theology, and history of dogma. But the same book testifies to the unworkable character of his understanding of the New Testament both (1) for Christian believers (because he so radically reinterpreted New Testament documents as to deny historic Christianity any empirically justifiable grounding in those documents) and (2) for other scholars who then and now detected and detect many failures in his approach and conclusions.

For example, Notger Slenzka stresses (p. 67) Baur's interpretation of the Reformation as the affirmation of radical individuality ('Selbstverhältnis'; lit. 'relationship to the self'; cf. p. 66: 'Autonomie des Subjekts') rather than, e.g., affirmation of theological truths, or revolutionary insight into the meaning of Romans 1:17 in line with Luther's testimony to that effect,[32] or union with Christ under his lordship. Any of these is plausible, but freedom of the self to be itself is surely anachronistic and mistaken. Baur's interpretation comports with his view of history as the self-realization of the idea of universal subjective freedom. But it has little to do with what can be documented in the writings of the Reformers.[33]

Here is a reminder of something much more plausible about how the Reformation got rolling. Historian Brian Cummings was recently reading Luther's actual handwritten notes on Romans written in 1515 and 1516, the year before the Ninety-Five Theses were posted. What does he detect steering Luther? It's a fascinating story:

> [Luther] reads the text in front of him and goes where it goes, even when this is into obscure and difficult places. One example, buried deep in his manuscript, is the distinction between 'active' and 'passive' *iustitia*. Using Jerome's Latin translation, he cites Romans 4:8, where Paul quotes from the Psalms: … (Blessed are those to whom the Lord imputes no sin/guilt).

---

32. See Brian Cummings, 'Luther in the Berlinka,' *Times Literary Supplement*, December 12, 2017.

33. Baur was not the last Pauline scholar to mishandle both Paul and Reformers. See Stephen J. Chester, *Reading Paul with the Reformers: Reconciling Old and New Perspectives* (Grand Rapids: Eerdmans, 2017); Robert Cara, *Cracking the Foundation of the New Perspective on Paul: Covenantal Nomism versus Reformed Covenantal Theology* (Fearn, Ross-shire, U.K.: Christian Focus/Mentor, 2017).

He begins with a new heading, *Expositio psalmi*. In the margin, he adds, 'Reuchlin'. To understand Paul's reading of the Psalms, the Latin language, and even Paul's Greek, are no longer enough; he interjects a line from the great Hebrew scholar, Johannes Reuchlin. Luther quotes and then underlines Reuchlin's rendering of the grammar of Hebrew, letter by letter:… (blessed is he who is relieved of sin). The Hebrew makes him see something which the Greek does not: that the construction is grammatically passive. Luther's text darkens here with the interruption of second thoughts: there are crossings out, additions above the line, sometimes second additions. And then in a moment of scribal clarity come the words: 'sed per deum active et in se passive levatur' (he is relieved actively by God and passively in himself). Word for word this is almost exactly what he wrote in the 1545 Preface [to his Latin works]: *iustitia dei* is not active but passive. With some passion, and sour humour, he adds that the philosophers and the jurists have got it wrong. For a moment he descends into German: 'o Sawtheologen': you pig-ignorant scholastics. Again, in 1545 he repeats that the philosophers have made a category error. But the idea comes not from philosophy lessons in the schools of Erfurt, but from reading, in noting how Hebrew and Greek and Latin mean things in different ways. In a profound way, Hebrew grammar changed the course of European history.[34]

The text of Scripture, and the hand of God saving a lost monk, lie at the root of the Reformation. This is precisely the kind of insight that Baur's commitments blind him to, even if he had had access to Luther's manuscript.

Back to the recent book on Baur, an insightful piece by Anders Gerdmar (featured in the previous chapter of this book), 'Baur and the Creation of the Judaism-Hellenism Dichotomy,' counters the almost hagiographic tendencies of some chapters of the book. He subjects Baur to scrutiny regarding his role in the creation of a historiography that turned out to be as destructive as it was dubious. He suggests much of Baur's outlook is rooted not only in 'Hegelian-like historiography' but in a social-political movement in Germany and Baur's own German territory of Württemberg. This movement 'housed nationalist, as well as emancipatory ideas, but also dreams of German greatness, and, on the other side, negative views about Jewish influence on Germany' (p. 124). Gerdmar shows that key aspects of Baur's views were furnished by his

---

34. Cummings, 'Luther in the Berlinka,' *Times Literary Supplement*, December 12, 2017.

anti-Jewish as well as anti-Catholic social setting, not by biblical exegesis or native genius. The next chapter, by Volker Henning Drecoll, is less critical of Baur than Gerdmar, yet goes so far as to raise the question whether Baur's historiography does not promote but actually sacrifices its 'critical' status and undermines theology's historical nature (p. 160).

Christof Landmesser analyzes Baur as an interpreter of Paul. This full and rich account majors on exposition but is not without critical insights, like Baur's downplaying of eschatology (p. 194). Pauline interpreters today recognize how vital Paul's understanding of last things was for all he preached and taught. Baur viewed his brand of historical criticism not as one way, but the *only* way, 'to grasp and conceptualize the actual content of the NT texts and of the Christian tradition' (p. 162). Here Baur's absolutist elitism comes into view.

If Baur had affirmed historic Christian convictions, his hermeneutical dogmatism would today draw withering fire if noted at all, but his allegiance to liberal convictions still popular among academics earns him defense and praise instead, as Robert Morgan's chapter 'Baur's New Testament Theology' demonstrates. Morgan registers occasional criticism (e.g., p. 268: 'Baur underestimated the importance of the Old Testament for Christian faith and theology,' a considerable understatement). He brilliantly dissects differences between Baur, confessional Christian conviction, and 'late modern and post-modern theologies' in the air today, so that his essay is one of the high points of the book. Yet his fundamental sympathy with Baur's break with supernatural Christianity (which Baur affirmed in his earliest scholarship; p. 292) is clear.

Less clear is Morgan's talk of Baur's 'orthodox belief in the central importance of Jesus for Christianity' (p. 277). Actually, as Stefan Alkier notes, Baur's 'binary logic of a seamless understanding of reality governed by cause and effect' demotes the New Testament's 'miracles including the miracle of Jesus' resurrection' to fiction (p. 308). A non-resurrected Jesus, as well as a human but not also divine Jesus, can be of central importance to a religion, but not to historic confessional Christianity.

We can be grateful for the appearance of a book that updates current understanding of Baur. For many concur, as James Carleton Paget in his essay 'The Reception of Baur in Britian' states, that 'the study of Christian origins after Baur is no more than a series of corrective footnotes' (p. 337). Baur has decidedly affected New Testament interpretation and deserves to be respected. Yet from a Christian standpoint he also needs to be recognized as a heterodox elite interpreter who has done much to normalize and legitimize scholarly interpretation of the New Testament that is allegorical unless we accept his negative verdict on matters like miracles, the incarnation, the resurrection, and much else that is central to robust Christian confession.

His massive, elaborate, but unconvincing argument for non-Pauline authorship of the Pastorals is a microcosmic case in point.[35] In this 150 page essay appearing in 1835, Baur deconstructs Pauline authorship of 1-2 Timothy and Titus and interprets them as describing second century events – 1 Timothy 2, for example, Baur interprets as a pseudo-Pauline response to Marcion, viz., as something that arose around A.D. 140.[36] He concludes by ridiculing as specious fabrication the historic Christian affirmation of Paul's authorship of the pastorals, Peter's authorship of his two canonical letters, and the entire scenario of Acts' historicity followed by a second Roman imprisonment and then Paul's and Peter's executions under Nero as attested in post-apostolic sources.[37] This means Baur empties the apostolic era of almost all the apostolic letters regarded as witnesses to pre-A.D. 70 circumstances and makes them rather testimony to his elaborate alternate history of strife extending out to nearly A.D. 200 to which he imagines the New Testament documents testify. If it seems shocking that I cast Baur as an allegorizer, it is only fair to point out that he first made that charge against over eighteen centuries of Christian understanding of its Scriptures and their historical, apostolic origins.

Stefan Alkier brings out the pastoral pathos of Baur's approach to the Bible's miracles as well as the populist-elitist division to which he contributes. In part due to Baur's negative verdict on miracles, in line with Spinoza and many others, 'the laity [viz., populist believers] are vexed by the miracle accounts embedded in worship service [Bible readings] which they are given no help in understanding. ... Sometimes they are even dissuaded from the Christian faith. Worse still, pastors are no longer sure what they can justifiably say at the graveside. Take away

---

35. F. C. Baur, *Die sogenannten Pastoralbriefe des Apostels Paulus aus neue kritisch untersucht* (Stuttgart and Tübingen: J. G. Cotta, 1835). Rpt. 2006 by Adamant Media Corporation in the Elibron Classics series.

36. Ibid., pp. 40-2.

37. Ibid., p. 144.

miracles and Easter faith is over with; then all you have at the graveside is silence' (pp. 309-10).

It is worth noting the respective heavenly hopes attested to by F. C. Baur's grave marker when contrasted with the tombstone of an equally brilliant and prolific New Testament scholar who viewed the biblical documents as early and authentic.[38] The first tombstone, that of Baur, gives no suggestion of Christian identity or heavenly hope, unless it would be the deceased's title *Dr Theologiae*.

The second, that of Adolf Schlatter, calls the observer to core Christian themes and to the Scriptures. The Bible verse on the cross is from John 7:37 of the Luther translation: 'Wen da dürstet, der komme zu mir und trinke!' English Bible readers know it in this form: 'If anyone thirsts, let him come to me and drink'.

Delving into Baur's freshly translated New Testament theology is a project for another day. I wrestled with it in its German form for many months in my doctoral studies and in some respects learned German from reading it. My largely negative assessment is found in my book

---

38. I am indebted to Dr Patrick Egan (pictured next to Schlatter's grave) for the photos.

The Salvation Historical Fallacy?[39] But let us now turn to one of Baur's most famous, if indirect, ideological heirs.

2.3 New Interest in Rudolf Bultmann (1884–1976)

A 2017 article by Charles W. Hedrick, based on his 2014 book *The Wisdom of Jesus*, sounds an oft-heard elitist theme that the faith and teaching of many if not most Christian churches are not rooted in Jesus or His teaching.[40] The sayings attributed to Jesus in the Gospels are not His but were made up by prophets speaking in His name generations later. The real Jesus is not the believed-in Jesus spoken of in Acts and the New Testament letters. The church is a social institution not envisioned by Jesus, and Jesus' radical ethic is replaced in the New Testament by bland Greco-Roman household codes. To sum up Hedrick's position I quote him: 'Jesus, the historical man, was merely a presupposition for the faith of the church. To judge from their creeds, all the church needed from Jesus was that he be born and die. His teaching and deeds were of no interest at all. The church's faith is not actually based on Jesus. ...'[41]

If any of this sounds familiar, it is perhaps because the first sentence of Rudolf Bultmann's *Theology of the New Testament* reads: 'The message of Jesus is a presupposition for the theology of the New Testament rather than a part of that theology itself.'[42] Indeed, Bultmann's name appears in the first paragraph of Hedrick's article, and Hedrick's points all reflect Bultmann's convictions, claims, and outlook.

Bultmann is widely regarded as the single most important New Testament scholar since the Enlightenment. His views as Hedrick reaffirms them in 2017 articulate the elitist verdict on a book and a faith understood very differently by populist Christianity. Let us note just a few places where Bultmann, long dead and for a couple of decades relegated to obscurity in many quarters, is now making a comeback and serving as a fresh inspiration for elitist outlooks.

---

39. See especially chapter 1.

40. Charles Hedrick, 'The Church's Gospel and the Idiom of Jesus,' *The Fourth R* 30/4 (2017) pp. 3-7, 26.

41. Ibid., p. 26.

42. Rudolf Bultmann, *Theology of the New Testament*, trans. Kendrick Grobel (New York: Charles Scribner's Sons, 1951), 1:3.

First, Southern Baptists deserve their share of credit here. The late Morris Ashcraft (1923–2011), a theologian at Southeastern Seminary who resigned as dean in 1987 when conservative trustees forced the resignation there of President W. Randall Lolly and called the faculty back to the truth of the Bible,[43] published a book on Bultmann in 1972 in the series Makers of the Modern Theological Mind. I recall perusing the book in the early 1980s, when Bultmann was a major focus of my doctoral studies. I did not make use of the book because I did not find any critical interaction with Bultmann, just exposition of his writings, which I did not need because I was reading Bultmann in German, and commendation of his views, which I found inexplicable given Bultmann's rejection of historic Christianity.

Ashcraft's book was reprinted in 2016 by Hendrickson. Apparently there is a fresh market for advocacy of Bultmann's ideas. This is confirmed by a string of publications, a mere trace of which I will mention. One is by philosopher of religion Tim Labron, *Bultmann Unlocked*, appearing in 2011.[44] This book attempts a positive retrieval of Bultmann by reading him with the help of Derrida and Wittgenstein. It unwisely rejects the scholarship of Bultmann's peers, many of whom rigorously and devastatingly critiqued any number of his publications and claims.[45]

A major impetus to current interest in Bultmann is the appearance of a comprehensive Bultmann biography. First published in German in 2009,[46] it made its English appearance in 2012.[47] The book is well-informed and voluminous but is thin on critical analysis. One could argue that criticism is not a biography's place. But a central reason for Bultmann's importance is his success at enthroning a reading of the New Testament that openly rejects all the text's central material transcendent claims concerning a knowable God's active personal presence and work

---

43. See '2 Resign Baptist Seminary in a Theology Dispute,' *New York Times*, October 24, 1987.

44. London: T&T Clark, 2011.

45. Note my review in *Themelios* 39/3 (November 2014).

46. Konrad Hammann, *Rudolf Bultmann – Eine Biographie* (Tübingen: Mohr Siebeck, 2009). Remarks on this book above draw on my review in *Bulletin of Biblical Research* 20/1 (2010) pp. 142-4. Parenthetical page numbers in this section refer to the German edition of Hammann's biography.

47. *Rudolf Bultmann: A Biography*, trans. Philip E. Devenish (Salem, OR: Polebridge, 2012).

in the world (e.g., miracles including Jesus' resurrection). Bultmann had a huge effect in the destruction of confidence in the Gospels in German universities.

For example, when Bultmann began his professorship at Marburg in 1921, his colleague Rudolf Otto argued for the genuineness of all the synoptic miracle accounts (p. 130). Less than a decade later Bultmann had published his book *Jesus and the Word* in which he displayed extreme skepticism of the New Testament's and our knowledge of Jesus. In Bultmann's lifetime, and to an extent through his influence, confidence in the Gospels' historicity by German biblical professors was dramatically reduced, with ripple effects across the whole spectrum of New Testament interpretation and reverberations in other disciplines like theology, as well as repercussions worldwide wherever German theological influence was felt.

Hammann does little beyond chronicle Bultmann's personal rejection of historic Christian faith from an early age (pp. 10-11), following in the footsteps of his pastor father, who under the influence of Ernst Troeltsch (p. 4) moved from a biblical and confessional stance to liberalism. (Bultmann's mother, however, remained faithful to historic Christianity: pp. 4-6.) As a student at Berlin, Bultmann complained in a letter about dogmatics lectures from Julius Kaftan, 'What rubbish is contained in terms like "revelation," "Trinity," "miracle," "God's attributes" – it's appalling!' (p. 23). The sea change in cultural mood that took place in Bultmann's time from the intellectual viability of creedal Christian conviction to its virtual banishment from professorial cognitive conviction is a bigger part of Bultmann's biography than this study acknowledges.

A central feature of his professional existence was rejection of his hermeneutic and its entailments by any number of equally proficient and intelligent scholars. Yet names like fellow New Testament scholars Oscar Cullmann and Leonhard Goppelt (who at a synodal meeting in Hannover in 1954 stated that a ministerial candidate holding Bultmann's view could not in good conscience take Lutheran ordination vows[48]) do not even appear in the index. The tendency is to lionize Bultmann

---

48. See Goppelt, 'Die Authorität der Heiligen Schrift und die Bibelkritik,' in *Wort Gottes und Bekenntnis*, Sonderdruck zur Rüstzeit der 15. ordentlichen Landessynode in Loccum (Pattensen 1954).

and trivialize Christian objections to his proposals. Hammann does recognize the central question (p. 422-3): 'In what relation could and should Protestant Christianity understand itself over against current secular conviction definitively marked by the Enlightenment?' But the only answers given are Bultmann's. Hammann makes all dissenters sound like anti-intellectuals on an ill-informed witch hunt. Doubtless some were, but many were not. Out of over two hundred monographs listed in the bibliography (pp. 520-7), only six are in English, and none is fundamentally critical of Bultmann. Plenty could have been cited.

Following this biography, Hammann in 2016 published a collection of eleven of his essays as the book *Rudolf Bultmann and His Time.*[49] This documents the ongoing interest in and influence of Bultmann. While Hammann asserts that for Bultmann 'academic dialog with foreign scholars was … an indispensable component of his theological existence' (p. 13), out of the hundreds of references to scholars and scholarship in this book's index of names, there is a total of three references to English-speaking scholars: Arthur Darby Nock (English), James M. Robinson, and E. P. Sanders (both Americans) each garner one mention. It is as if English-language scholarship on Bultmann does not exist. Hammann does make reference to Anders Gerdmar's important study *Roots of Theological Anti-Semitism. German Biblical Interpretation and the Jews, from Herder and Semler to Kittel and Bultmann* (2009), but only to disparage and dismiss it in a footnote (pp. 53 n. 65; see also 75 n. 198).[50] There is no reference to Gerdmar in the index. The fact is that while Bultmann gladly acknowledged plaudits and renown from abroad, his substantial interaction with contemporary non-German scholarship was negligible.

A welcome contribution of this volume lies in its insight into numerous finer, often quite important, and always interesting points relating to Bultmann's experiences, outlook, and contribution. Where did Bultmann get the idea of looking for insight into the Fourth Gospel prologue from the (much later) Mandaean writings? From the Old Testament scholar Hermann Gunkel (pp. 20-1). Which publisher at first gave Bultmann's first widely known book, *Die Geschichte der synoptischen*

---

49. *Rudolf Bultmann und seine Zeit: Biographische und theologische Konstellationen* (Tübingen: Mohr Siebeck, 2016). Parenthetical page references in the next two paragraphs are to this work.

50. Leiden: Brill, 2010.

Tradition, a rejection slip? The Göttingen publisher Gustav Ruprecht (pp. 25-6). Which words or sayings of Jesus did Bultmann think most likely to be authentic? See the seventy-six passages embedded in a letter from Bultmann to Gunkel, who had asked Bultmann for his top forty probably-most-genuine sayings (pp. 35-40). When did Bultmann reject historic Christian faith, like that possessed by his mother, a faith which affirms 'orthodox' belief like 'personal trust in the miraculous work of the savior' (p. 4)? This probably took place in conjunction with (1) his exposure to modern thought in high school and (2) his pastor father's shift from confessional to liberal conviction (ibid.).

One other, quite new major German work bears mention: Christof Landmesser, ed., *Bultmann Handbuch*.[51] By appearing in Mohr Siebeck's 'Handbücher Theologie' series that began in 2008 and that also offers volumes on Calvin, Athanasius, Paul, Barth, Thomas Aquinas, Luther, Jesus, and Schleiermacher, we see that Bultmann now appears on this publisher's Mount Rushmore with nine other faces, among them Jesus'.

This scholarly tool and tribute is not uncritical of its subject. Thomas Dörken-Kucharz faults Bultmann for a faulty, idealist, and bourgeois notion of culture that was already being rejected in the universities in the 1920s. Yet Bultmann held on to it (p. 172). While Martin Bauspieß appears to defend Bultmann against the charge of ahistoricity in his theology (pp. 322-3), he at least acknowledges telling objections from Oscar Cullmann, Wolfhart Pannenberg, and Heinrich Ott. Ulrich H. J. Körtner shows that Bultmann's theology *was* ultimately ahistorical: he reduces the truth of the kerygma merely to an individual's subjectivity. Körtner observes: 'The basis for this truth claim however remains circular in the framework of [Bultmann's] word-of-God theology' (p. 367). Despite these and many other criticisms of Bultmann, the general conclusion is that Bultmann's numerous weaknesses in the light of subsequent research do not call in question his contribution toward 'a theological and existential relevance for exegetical theology'. On the contrary, 'Bultmann's work ... remains an exemplary model' (p. 453). It seems we can expect continued and perhaps increasing influence of Bultmann in German New Testament interpretation and theology.

---

51. Handbücher Theologie (Tübingen: Mohr Siebeck, 2017). Parenthetical page references in the next paragraph are to this work.

This judgment is confirmed by German New Testament theologian Peter Stuhlmacher. In assessing his life's work in biblical theology at Tübingen University, he recalls the synergy between his work and that of colleagues including Harmut Gese, Otto Betz, Martin Hengel, Gert Jeremias, and Otfried Hofius.[52] But he laments that the current Tübingen faculty is not carrying on in this direction but is rather 'once again turning to the perspectives of the Bultmann school'.[53]

Currently a major voice pushing Bultmann in the English-language setting is David W. Congdon, with works including *The Mission of Demythologizing: Rudolf Bultmann's Dialectical Theology*,[54] and *The God Who Saves: A Dogmatic Sketch*.[55] The former concludes that Bultmann and the dialectical theology Congdon derives from his work are the means to demythologize *everything* in theology, including God, and therefore realize the real Christian message. In the second book Congdon gives his testimony of moving from being a Wheaton College (IL) student about fifteen years ago to an ardent universalist now.[56] There is no hell.[57] Everyone in all times will be saved, and this truth is justified from Bultmann's dialectical theology. Congdon pronounces this dialectical theology to be 'exegetically grounded and existentially concerned' and therefore 'the realization of genuinely *evangelical* theology'.[58] He concludes his massive *The Mission of Demythologizing* with these words: 'While many view his work as a relic from the last century incapable of speaking to the church at the present time, perhaps Bultmann's day is still to come.'[59] If Congdon's views have a future, so do Bultmann's, as Congdon relies substantially on the Bultmannian synthesis.

---

52. Peter Stuhlmacher, 'Die Tübinger Biblische Theologie des Neuen Testaments – ein Rückblick,' *Theologische Beiträge* 48 (2017) pp. 76-91.

53. Daniel Bailey, 'Translator's Preface,' in Peter Stuhlmacher, *Biblical Theology of the New Testament* (Grand Rapids: Baker, 2018), xvii n. 9.

54. Minneapolis: Fortress, 2015.

55. Eugene, OR: Cascade, 2016.

56. The Wheaton College Statement of Faith affirms: 'WE BELIEVE in the bodily resurrection of the just and unjust, the everlasting punishment of the lost, and the everlasting blessedness of the saved.' See https://www.wheaton.edu/about-wheaton/statement-of-faith-and-educational-purpose/, accessed June 29, 2018.

57. *The God Who Saves*, p. 263.

58. Ibid., xviii n. 7.

59. *Mission of Demythologizing*, p. 836.

3. Conclusion

In this chapter we have revisited and refined the definitions of elitist and populist, terms important in this book's overarching theme. We have also documented and characterized the enduring appeal of what I have called neo-allegorical interpretation as found in two of the last two centuries' most influential 'elitist' interpreters, F. C. Baur and Rudolf Bultmann. Their approach to New Testament interpretation despite the negative verdict of their convictions on historic Christianity appear to be gaining fresh impetus at the same time that populist expansion calls for rethinking of the elitist hegemony. Is there any rapprochement possible between these two disparate strands? That will be, in part, the topic of the next chapter.

To conclude this one I draw again on Ulrich Wilckens, a scholar mentioned in chapter one who late in life has turned on German New Testament theology and written two books critiquing it. Baur and Bultmann are among many in his crosshairs. Lest the remarks above be thought to seem too negative and pessimistic, here is a distillation of his objections and a pointer toward an antidote to Baur's and Bultmann's failings.

Regarding Baur,[60] Wilckens questions his vaunted 'purely historical' commitment. In Wilckens' view, Baur simply excludes *a priori* all theological aspects of New Testament texts. What is left is not what the text says but what in Baur's judgment was the effect that the writer tries to produce. Baur called this *Tendenz*, which can be understood as the hidden motive, bias, or agenda of the writer. To interpret a New Testament book so that its *Tendenz* is revealed, after its plain meaning had been set aside, was part one of Baur's 'historical' interpretation.

Part two was his commitment to the underlying idea which was at the root of Christianity's development and which comes to the fore in the documents associated with its rise. Here Baur drew on Hegel's dialectic, in which history can be understood as thesis, antithesis, and synthesis, which synthesis then serves as thesis to a subsequent interaction.

Both conservative and so-called critical interpreters of Baur's time objected to his crass imposition of idealistic philosophy on New

---

60. The next two paragraphs draw on Wilckens, *Historische Kritik der historisch-kritischen Exegese*, pp. 248-9.

Testament history and theology.[61] This peaks in his final work, *Lectures on New Testament Theology*. Baur commends the Sermon on the Mount as the essence of what Jesus brought. In antithesis to Judaism, Jesus set forth Kant's categorical imperative. Jesus was not the Messiah but came rather to commend the purely ethical disposition of love for neighbor in place of sinful self-centeredness.[62]

It is hard to imagine an approach less user-friendly to a Christian reading of Scripture, but Wilckens' verdict on Bultmann is if anything more pessimistic. While he gives credit where he can, in the end he groups him with Barth and notes that in Germany regard for their dialectical theology came to a screeching halt over a generation ago.[63] Wilckens locates their weakness in the failure of theology in general for over one hundred years now to represent God as more than an abstraction. He comments that all theologians claim to point to God somehow, but with Barth what you're left with at most is the idea of the divine as the 'entirely other', and with Bultmann 'the word of God in the kerygma'. Laments Wilckens: 'The theological *reality* of what they both present remains, basically, mere assertion. No wonder the effect is so negligible on people of our time.'[64]

What Wilckens calls for is the courage to return to confession of Christ crucified and risen, in connection with taking seriously as historical reality 'God in the wondrousness [Wunderbarkeit] of his action.'[65] Our next chapter will explore ways populist testimony might steer us in that direction.

61. Ibid., pp. 254-5.

62. Ibid., p. 257.

63. Ibid., p. 343.

64. Ibid., p. 344. Arriving at an analogously pessimistic assessment of Bultmann and Barth from a (Swiss) German perspective years earlier was Klaus Bockmühl, *The Unreal God of Modern Theology: Bultmann, Barth, and the Theology of Atheism* (Colorado Springs, CO: Helmers & Howard Publishers, 1988).

65. Ibid.

CHAPTER THREE

Is Rapprochement[1] Possible ... or Even Relevant?

1. Review and the Status Quo

In chapter one I called attention to uneasy relations between what I have been terming populist understanding of Scripture, on the one hand, and elitist, on the other. Why is this even an issue?

It is an issue because we inhabit a world in which for over two centuries a subgroup associated with the Western Protestant church has assumed and asserts control of the meaning of the Bible (as exemplified by James Kelhoffer's response to Anders Gerdmar described in chapter one), promulgated a skeptical understanding of its history and message, and exerted profound influence on pastoral training and cultural perception of the truth of the Bible, not only in the West but worldwide. While churches embracing some version of this hermeneutic of skepticism have tanked in membership numbers and are increasingly complicit in a social order that denigrates pre-Enlightenment Christianity and its correlates today and supports practices like abortion and sexual immorality, God has been saving tens of millions of people worldwide who have believed the saving message that in elitist understanding is invalid, at least for cultured people among whom they dwell.

I note that German New Testament scholar Jörg Frey has conceded that the classic Western 'historical-critical' paradigm does not bear the same binding hermeneutical authority 'in other cultural contexts', so that in those contexts 'other approaches can in increasing measure be

---

1. Defined as establishing or resuming harmonious relations.

regarded as more or less legitimate'.[2] He calls such approaches, however, 'dezidiert nicht historisch[e] Ansätz[e]' ('categorically not historical approaches'). How does he know? Has he examined them all? The most likely reason he can make that vast generalization is that he probably correctly assumes they are not 'the' elitist-sanctioned approach called *historisch-kritisch* by those who consider it normative. Frey does correctly speak of 'Spannung' here – 'tension.'

I thought it fitting to explore this tension, which I did particularly through commentary on the exchange (in chapter one) between biblical interpreters in Sweden on opposite sides of the issue, because thoughtful interpreters of Scripture today are often affected by both worlds. For all concerned it is important to be aware of ultimate loyalties and the warrants we claim for them.

In chapter two, after further defining features of populism and elitism, I looked at the resurgence of interest in F. C. Baur and Rudolf Bultmann, who are among the most revered and influential paragons of elitist method and outlook in the field of New Testament theology, with effects far beyond. This resurgence suggests that at least some in the elitist hegemony are more apt to mine models of the past, and failed models at that many think, than they are to reconsider the view of God which, Ulrich Wilckens argues, has gone sour now for several generations with unhappy results for New Testament theology.

That leads to the present chapter: 'Is Rapprochement Possible … or Even Relevant?' The answer to the first part, is rapprochement possible, is easy from the elitist side: no! We saw in chapter one that at least in the Kelhoffer-Gerdmar debate, there is a core of consensus guild conviction apart from which intellectually responsible interpretation of the Bible is disparaged unless it conforms to what the last two hundred years of criticism are taken to have established. Gerdmar discovered this by publishing his book arguing for a Protestant or evangelical interpretation of Scripture and salvation in contrast to Roman Catholic belief. And I indicated in chapter two, based on elitist exegesis and reasoning, there is no place either for historic consensual Christian understanding of Scripture in the Baur-Bultmann heritage. David Congdon highlighted

---

2. Jörg Frey, *Von Jesus zur neutestamentlichen Theologie: Kleine Schriften II*, ed. B. Schliesser, Wissenschaftliche Untersuchungen zum Neuen Testament 368 (Tübingen: Mohr Siebeck, 2016), 52 n. 108.

this by parlaying his synthesis of Barth and Bultmann to confirm elimination of the existence of hell,[3] indicating his doubt of something of which the canonical Jesus seemed to be harrowingly sure. He also eliminates belief in a conscious afterlife generally,[4] drawing on Barth and Eberhard Jüngel.

I want to bore just a little deeper here. Based on Barth and Jüngel, while Congdon concedes that people want assurance of life in the here-after, he writes that 'ministers of the gospel should avoid claiming that we will see our loved ones in heaven'.[5] The idea of Jesus going to prepare a place for His followers (John 14:3) or being with them this very day in Paradise (Luke 23:43) or eating together 'at the feast in the kingdom of God' (Luke 14:15 NIV), or in the old hymn's words 'when we all get to heaven we'll sing and shout the victory'[6] – all such notions stem, Congdon argues, from an individualist stage in evolving human social consciousness that in the elitist understanding we have now transcended.

The Psalmist's words, 'I am for peace; but when I speak, they are for war' (Ps. 120:7) seem to apply for the Christian who wants to uphold notions like Jesus Christ's bodily resurrection, His return in judgment and glory, and the gathering of God's people to Him for an age to come of conscious personal and social life in and for the Triune God. Not on elitism's watch! 'It is time that theologians directly and honestly address these matters,' Congdon says. On Congdon's reading following from Bultmann's (and Barth's and Ebeling's and Gollwitzer's and Jüngel's),[7] rapprochement with the faith which populists affirm was once for all delivered to the saints (Jude 3) is securely behind us, replaced by updates that are unrecognizable as either biblical or Christian by historic consensual standards.

2. Populist Harvest and Hope

It is my hope and contention that we are on the verge of a time when the populist harvest that has seen hundreds of millions added to

---

3. *The God Who Saves*, p. 263.

4. Ibid., pp. 262-74.

5. Ibid., p. 274.

6. *Baptist Hymnal* (Nashville: Convention Press, 1975), p. 491.

7. Congdon, *The God Who Saves*, xviii.

church memberships will result in fruit in the form of reclamation of biblical hermeneutics for Christ and His kingdom in parts of the world where elitist interpretation has gained undue sway. I believe something went wrong when Western European and gradually North American churches put what has become the elitist synthesis over biblical exegesis and theological reflection and then inflicted the results on ministerial training. The results are clear to see in the wreckage of the Protestant mainline in North America[8] and the catastrophic social results not just for churches but for a whole nation as traced, e.g., in Joseph Bottum's important book *An Anxious Age*.[9]

Theological conservatives in a place like the U.S. have nothing to crow about, because our churches and ethos have tended to settle ever lower in the Western secular morass in which we are thrashing in search of solid ground. We are in much need of repentance and spiritual transfusion from the world Christian upsurge as elitists are. According to Gregory A. Wills, as recently as the late 1980s, the president of the largest Southern Baptist seminary and 'most moderate leaders' in the Southern Baptist denomination (the largest Protestant group in the U.S.) 'believed that an inerrantist scholar was an oxymoron, a practical impossibility since intelligent and informed persons could not rationally believe in inerrancy.'[10] Yet inerrancy was and remains the view of Scripture held by most of the church through most of its history. Yes; I said still is: I'll explain that below. It is a sign of elitist malaise infecting Western evangelical conviction that the authority of Scripture has been embattled in its own ranks for about the last hundred years, stretching back another hundred years in some circles.

But there may be a way to stop the descent. So I will now list some reasons why there is hope for a populist approach to Scripture, Christian faith, and lived-out life by those with the wisdom and will to see through

---

8. The literature is vast. For a lament of liberal Presbyterian directions of a generation ago, see John H. Leith, *Crisis in the Church: The Plight of Theological Education* (Louisville: Westminster John Knox, 1997). See also Thomas Oden, *Requiem: A Lament in Three Movements* (Nashville: Abingdon, 1995).

9. New York: Image, 2014.

10. Gregory A. Wills, *Southern Baptist Seminary 1859-2009* (Oxford: Oxford University Press, 2009), p. 478.

elitist pretensions and the decadent populism to which I have repeatedly called attention, especially on these U.S. shores.

2.1 Continued and Increasing Scholarly Engagement

There is hope for a populist approach to Scripture, Christian faith, and lived-out life first because of academic evangelical involvement already underway. The church has always flourished, when it has, with the aid of world-class exegetes and theologians. Well-trained, intellectually capable leaders were used by God to steer the church for its first 1800 years and since, and it is elitist misrepresentation to imply, as histories of interpretation normally do, that no one really thought critically until Enlightenment skepticism of biblical truth claims wormed its way in and displaced traditional exegesis, theological reasoning, church leadership, and eventually ministerial training. While there is much to lament in Western evangelicalism at all levels, there is much to affirm too, and that includes its significant injection of a Christian voice in academic circles and guilds worldwide. The Carl F. H. Henry Center at Trinity Evangelical Divinity School has this statement posted on its website:

> The evangelical movement is at its best when it resists the temptation of ecclesial or intellectual isolationism, and instead actively engages both the wider Christian world and the intellectual problems that face the church. It is this kind of evangelicalism that Henry championed, and it is this ethos that the Henry Center has sought to preserve and promote.[11]

The Henry Center, Trinity Evangelical Divinity School, and likeminded institutions of higher learning around the world conduct and sponsor scholarship that both contributes to the nourishment of their Bible-believing constituencies and results in published offerings that represent a historic Christian viewpoint in social locations where elitist convictions are often the norm. In that sense the answer to this chapter's question, is rapprochement possible?, is yes, because there is a certain fraternal tie and concourse between the two.

If you read *National Geographic*, you will be accustomed to articles and asides that are not always friendly to Christian convictions. But

---

11. http://henrycenter.tiu.edu/2018/01/a-modern-creature-introducing-a-conversation/. Accessed January 29, 2019.

thanks to the stance and industry of evangelical scholarship, in the December 2017 issue an article called 'The Search for the Real Jesus' was actually fairly balanced. The reporter, Kristen Romey, does not refer to populist and elitist by those terms, but it's what she was observing as she wrote:

> Scholars who study Jesus divide into two opposing camps separated by a very bright line: those who believe the wonder-working Jesus of the Gospels is the real Jesus, and those who think the real Jesus – the man who inspired the myth – hides below the surface of the Gospels and must be revealed by historical research and literary analysis. Both camps claim archaeology as their ally, leading to some fractious debates and strange bedfellows.[12]

She later quotes a Baptist source:

> ... insights gleaned from excavations across Galilee have led to a significant shift in scholarly opinion, says Craig Evans, professor of Christian origins in the School of Christian Thought at Houston Baptist University. 'Thanks to archaeology, there's been a big change of thinking – from Jesus the cosmopolitan Hellenist to Jesus the observant Jew.'[13]

In many places one finds evangelical scholars embedded in discussions proceeding under elitist auspices – I think not only of places like *National Geographic* but of sessions at national SBL or AAR meetings where evangelicals are generally in the minority but make significant contributions.

Or take the *Encyclopedia of the Bible and Its Reception*. In its volume 14 article on Jesus (cols. 1-7), drawing on more evangelically aligned scholars like Craig Evans, Scot McKnight, and Stanley Porter, Tom Holmén adopts a populist rather than skeptical interpretation of the evidence: 'the picture the sources paint of Jesus stays broadly on target' (col. 1). Holmén points out in closing that 'where the scholarly [i.e., elitist] view of Jesus most clearly parts from the traditional [i.e. populist] Christian faith is in the interpretation of the outcome of Jesus' work' (col. 6). The 'scholarly view' would doubt the resurrection, whereas 'the followers of Jesus became convinced of' it. Jesus' vindication by God

---

12. Kristen Romey, 'The Search for the Real Jesus,' *National Geographic*, Dec. 2017 (232/6) p. 43.

13. Ibid., p. 60.

and His continuing life 'stretches his importance from the first century to our time and beyond' (col. 7). In the elitist view the resurrection is an ancient claim to a scientific impossibility and as such has no claim to importance in our time except perhaps as unfortunate continuing blind faith, as in Bultmann's demythologizing outlook.

Or just open a recent number of the journal called *New Testament Abstracts*.[14] On pages 390-391 there is notice of an article by Patrick Schreiner in *Currents in Biblical Research*, by Stanley E. Porter and Andrew Pitts in *Journal for the Study of the Historical Jesus*, and Elizabeth Y. Sung in *Ex Auditu*. Patrick Schreiner did his MDiv and PhD at Southern Baptist Theological Seminary. Porter and Pitts are associated with McMaster Divinity College in Canada, an evangelical college with Baptist roots. Sung is an evangelical scholar who trained with Kevin Vanhoozer at Trinity Evangelical Divinity School and was a professor there for some years.

There is hope for a populist approach to Scripture, as I have been defining it, affecting higher learning and conviction worldwide, because recent generations have seen the rise of a high level of scholarship in evangelical circles which have always been resistant to unchecked implementation of elitist trends and demands. If these Western evangelical ranks can continue to grow in number, sophistication, and positive connection with burgeoning world Christianity, and if Western evangelical churches can find renewal, for we need it, prospects for redemptive populism informed by high levels of scholarship will be enhanced.

2.2 Tenacity of Populist Conviction Even unto Death

A second reason for hope for a populist approach to Scripture, Christian faith, and lived-out life lies in the faithfulness unto death that God sometimes calls for and grants from those in populist ranks. Rather than redefine or evaporate the Christian hope as elitist skepticism tends to do, the populist approach is often to live it despite disincentives, to say yes wholly to Jesus' invitation when 'he said to all, "If anyone would come after me, let him deny himself and take up his cross daily and follow me"' (Luke 9:23). What does this look like? A photo may strike a chord. It was taken at the gravesite on

---

the hospital grounds, where both of the deceased had requested to be buried, were they to die in their daily full-time foreign mission service:[15]

Notice that both these people, William Edwin Koehn and Martha Crystal Myers, died the same day just over fifteen years ago. They were both Southern Baptists. And by every indication their conviction was populist as I have been defining it.

A press release at the time ran like this:

Slain Missionary, Dr Martha Myers,
'Gave Her All to People who Were Suffering'

BIRMINGHAM, Ala. – Dr Martha C. Myers, the Southern Baptist missionary shot to death by an extremist in Yemen Dec. 30, was remembered as a person 'mature beyond her years, especially in her Christian commitment,' by a former teacher.

Dr Mike Howell, her biology professor at Samford University, described Myers as a well-rounded person but one who was 'absolutely serious' about becoming a medical missionary.

'She was a brilliant, hard-working person, good in things other than biology,' he said. 'She sang in the A Cappella Choir and edited the literary magazine, but there was never any doubt among the faculty that she was headed to the medical mission field.'

---

15. I am indebted to my longtime friend Glen Land, who was at this site not long after the shooting, for this photograph.

Dr Myers graduated from Samford in 1967 and the University of Alabama Medical School in 1971. An obstetrician, she served at Jibla Baptist Hospital in Yemen for more than 25 years. ...

Myers was killed along with two other hospital staff members, administrator William Koehn and purchasing manager Kathleen Gariety. ...

Catherine Allen of Birmingham, [a] classmate [of Myers at Samford University], said Myers was 'very focused and very productive.' It was this focused personality and 'a distinct calling of God' that enabled Myers to serve for so long in Yemen, said Allen.

'The Yemen hospital was the most enduring, visible and viable International Mission Board witness in the Middle East,' said Allen, a former administrator of the Woman's Missionary Union.

Myers and Koehn were buried on the grounds of the hospital they had served for a quarter of a century.[16]

Thanks to a personal friend who visited Yemen shortly after Dr Myers' death I can add a little to this account, edited from my friend's personal journal.[17] Of the three murders that day, Martha was the target. She was an obstetrician/surgeon at the hospital. She died penniless, having sold her furniture and other possessions to give to the poor. She traveled all over the region inoculating children and caring for the sick. She had earlier befriended her killer's wife and had shared Christ with her. Consequently, he determined to kill her and planned the murder for many months. During this time he became associated with Al Qaeda. On the day of the killings he called the hospital and had Martha paged. This to assure that she would be at the telephone in the hospital office. He smuggled a pistol in with him, went straight to the office and shot and killed her. He then shot Bill Koehn, who was seated at the desk beside Martha and Kathy Gariety, who also happened to be in the office. He then went to the next room and shot the pharmacist, who would later recover.

16. https://www.samford.edu/news/2003/Slain-Missionary-Dr-Martha-Myers-Gave-Her-All-to-People-who-Were-Suffering, accessed on February 15, 2018. For a more recent reminiscence, see https://www.imb.org/2017/12/15/martyrs-jibla-baptist-hospital/, accessed February 15, 2018.

17. Rev. Glen A. Land, at that time State Missions Director, Minnesota-Wisconsin Baptist Convention of the Southern Baptist Convention.

In the wake of the attack, Bill Koehn's widow, Martha Koehn, continued to serve at the hospital where her husband and Martha Myers were buried.

My point here is not to suggest that the norm or necessity for populists is martyrdom. But it is to draw a contrast between two social subgroups in the world. One is elitist, whose vocation is, to repeat Lamin Sanneh's words, 'a domesticated activity of the mind'.[18] For many generations this subgroup has justified itself in part by the claim that they are advancing the truth, disabusing the simple of misguided faith in a substantially misleading corpus of ancient documents, and pointing in more enlightened intellectual, social, and perhaps religious directions. To my knowledge this is not a subgroup frequently subject to lethal persecution for its loyalty to the God and Christ of whom the Bible speaks. In some cases they acquire fame and status by their opposition to and undermining of such loyalty.[19]

The other subgroup, however, is populist Christian. They die, by the year, to the tune of some 90,000 annually. That's about ten Christians every hour of the day, 24/7.[20] While many may be nominal, Christians in name only and not by dint of personal commitment, many are not. Many times 90,000 per year live faithfully as Christians knowing that due to the part of the world they are living in and their commitment to life in Christ, they could lose their life on earth on any given day. I think of believers in places like Egypt and many other Near Eastern countries, Sudan and South Sudan, northern Nigeria, India, China,

---

18. Lamin Sanneh, *Whose Religion Is Christianity? The Gospel beyond the West* (Grand Rapids/Cambridge, U.K.: Eerdmans, 2003), pp. 57f.

19. For a trivialization of the persecution of Christians, see Candida Moss, *The Myth of Persecution: How Early Christians Invented a Story of Martyrdom* (San Francisco: HarperOne, 2013). For a telling review, see N. Clayton Croy, *Review of Biblical Literature* 10 (2013), pp. 1-6, available at https://www.bookreviews.org/pdf/9158_10095.pdf, accessed January 29, 2019. For a fresh treatment of persecution in the New Testament era, see Eckhard J. Schnabel, 'The Persecution of Christians in the First Century,' *Journal of the Evangelical Theological Society* 61.3 (2018), pp. 525-47.

20. Todd M. Johnson, Gina A. Zurlo, Albert W. Hickman, and Peter Crossing, 'Christianity 2017: Five Hundred Years of Protestant Christianity,' *International Bulletin of Missionary Research* 41/1 (January 2017), p. 50. For defense of the figure and its computation, see Todd M. Johnson, Gina A. Zurlo, Albert W. Hickman, and Peter F. Crossing, 'Christianity 2018: More African Christians and Counting Martyrs,' *International Bulletin of Missionary Research* 42/1 (January 2018), pp. 20-8.

and North Korea to name some primary hazardous locations. But these potential targets believe in what elitists like David Congdon counsel us we do not have: personal assurance of eternal life along with the important understanding that God does not leave the death of His loved ones unavenged.

Martyr-grade bravery may be rare in Western settings, but it is not unheard of. Hardly ten miles from where I write, on November 24, 2018, the question was posed, 'Will this be the first American-born woman martyr?' Thus ran the title of an op-ed article on a Roman Catholic website by Fr. Brian W. Harrison, O.S.[21] He was referring to the murder of Jamie Schmidt in Ballwin, Missouri, on November 19, 2018. Harrison noted that 'no American woman or lay person – and no U.S. citizen at all who died on this nation's soil – has so far been honored by the Church as a martyr.' He raised the question whether Schmidt should be so recognized.

The incident, perpetrated by the since-apprehended Thomas Bruce, is described by Harrison in words confirmed by many news sources. Bruce entered a Catholic religious supply store at mid-day when just three women were present. He ordered them to the back of the store. He began assaulting them sexually.

But Harrison brings out a religious dimension downplayed by both local and national journalists. The last of the three women to be attacked was

> ... Jamie Schmidt, 53, a quiet mother of three who worked as a secretarial assistant at the St Louis Community College in the western suburb of Wildwood, and was active in her parish church, St Anthony of Padua at High Ridge in neighboring Jefferson County. There was nothing obviously extraordinary about this lady. But now she did something very extraordinary indeed. Having just been forced to witness in horror the sexual assault of the two women beside her, Mrs Schmidt was ordered to submit to similar abuse. But Mrs Schmidt – shocked, defenseless, and with the barrel of a loaded gun pointed at her head – Just Said No.
>
> With death staring her in the face, Jamie quietly refused to allow her purity, her personal dignity, and her marriage covenant to be outraged. She looked him straight in the eye and said, 'In the name of God, I will not

---

21. https://www.lifesitenews.com/opinion/will-this-be-the-first-american-born-martyr. Accessed January 29, 2019.

take my clothes off.' Enraged by this unexpected point-blank rejection of his demand, her assailant responded with a point-blank shot that felled her on the spot. The survivor who gave this testimony added that as Jamie lay there gravely wounded, she could be heard whispering the words of the Our Father.

If confessing Christians who die in the name of God are attesting truly to the reality and the will of the God of Scripture revealed in Christ, it follows that the answer to this chapter's second question – is rapprochement even relevant? – is in an important sense no. The martyr church worldwide certainly outnumbers elitist theological scholars in this odd sense: more martyrs die annually (some 90,000; see above) than the number of elitist scholars existing in university and church graduate schools, certainly in the United States, perhaps in the entire West, and possibly worldwide. The martyr church is not asking scholars if they can affirm that Paul wrote Ephesians, that the Gospel words of Jesus are authentic, or that the one who is faithful unto death will receive the crown of life (Rev. 2:10). And people who are willing to die for their belief in the Bible's truth are not a subgroup shrinking but rather a communion continuing to grow at a remarkable rate.

It must be faced squarely that this raises questions for those who are populist but not (yet) martyrs: is our faith and response to God worthy of our being counted as belonging to the same body of Christ? And: if God continues to spare us from their ultimate level of sacrifice, what kind of changes are needed? Or are we like cows of Bashan at ease in Zion (Amos 4:1; 6:1)? For some of us who may have an appointment with death for Jesus' sake, how can we find and be true to that calling?

2.3 Populist Promise for New Testament Theology's Search for Truth

A third reason for hope for a populist approach to Scripture, Christian faith, and lived-out life is its viability for the enterprise of New Testament theology worthy of the name. Namely, it affirms a positive relation between salvation and history.

J. V. Fesko has spoken of 'two different types of biblical theology: historicocritical and redemptive-historical.' Geerhardus Vos (1862–1949) represents the latter, whereas a more skeptical scholar like Charles Briggs pursued the former, in 'an effort,' in Vos' words, 'to use the horizontal plane of history to neutralize the vertical plane of divine inspiration.'[22]

It is possible to view the whole history of New Testament theology as ongoing debate between these two perspectives. One line, the 'historicocritical,' starts with Baur,[23] modifies with William Wrede and the history of religion school, and finds fulfillment in Bultmann. It continues today in the works, e.g., of Heikki Räisänen, who finds the sacred not in Christian revelation but in (certain expressions of) human culture.[24] It may be termed the elitist line, reading the New Testament as if its theological claims are at best just matters some people believed back then and certainly not revealed truths about God with continuing force today.

Another line, the redemptive-historical, begins in the history of German New Testament theology with J. C. K. von Hofmann, a contemporary of Baur; continues with Adolf Schlatter, contemporary with Wrede; and echoes in the New Testament theological production of, among others, Oscar Cullmann, Leonhard Goppelt, George Ladd, Donald Guthrie, I. Howard Marshall, Frank Thielman, Ben Witherington III, Thomas Schreiner, and Craig Blomberg, all of whom offer alternatives to Bultmann. It may be termed salvation-historical, but in its hermeneutical orientation and characteristic theological claims this line is populist. It is a reading open to the New Testament's theological claims.

Johannes Zachhuber in his study of F. C. Baur notes the irony that the truth Baur sought was ruled out by his philosophical commitments, which 'all but excluded' what he claimed to be looking for, which Zachhuber characterizes as the unifying of fact and meaning in critical study of the New Testament and its history. He goes on to point out that there does not seem to be 'a ready solution forthcoming to the

22. J. V. Fesko, *The Spirit of the Age* (Grand Rapids: Reformation Heritage Books, 2017), p. 109, quoting Vos, 'The Idea of Biblical Theology as a Science and as a Theological Discipline,' in *Redemptive History and Biblical Interpretation*, p. 15).

23. For still earlier roots, see Otto Merk, *Biblische Theologie des Neuen Testaments in ihrer Anfangszeit: Ihre methodischen Probleme bei Johann Philipp Gabler und Georg Lorenz Bauer und deren Nachwirkungen* (Marburg: N. G. Elwert, 1972).

24. See Timo Eskola, *Beyond Biblical Theology: Sacralized Culturalism in Heikki Räisänen's Hermeneutics*, Biblical Interpretation 123 (Leiden: Brill, 2013). Note review by Michael Bird in *Review of Biblical Literature* 9 (2016).

fundamental systematic problems to which [Baur's] work testifies.' In fact, 'there is little evidence that the last 150 years have moved decisively beyond the aporiae that are brought out in Baur's work.'[25] I would observe here that when you rule out God's knowable saving hand from the witness of the Bible, New Testament or Old, it will be hard to convince others that you have an ultimate key to the meaning associated with the facts you find in the biblical writings. This is one reason why biblical studies is so fragmented in its methods and findings.

Chapter one pointed to a set of convictions affirmed by most of those whom I am calling populist:

1. a transcendent creator God
2. the Trinity
3. human and cosmic fallen-ness
4. the incarnation
5. the divinity of Christ
6. Christ's virgin birth, atoning death, and bodily resurrection
7. biblical miracles
8. the new birth through renewal by the Holy Spirit as the gospel is preached and received
9. the glorious visible and bodily return of Jesus Christ
10. eternal life and eternal punishment
11. an inspired authoritative Scripture that teaches us about all these things.

It is my contention that a set of convictions like these is a plausible representation of true assertions found in the Bible and valuable for ongoing synthetic analysis of the New Testament, which is how I would define New Testament theology. Populist conviction affirms the positive connection between salvation and history that the New Testament claims – e.g., 'But when the fullness of time had come [that's history], God sent forth his Son, born of woman, born under the law, to redeem those who were under the law, so that we might receive adoption as

---

25. Zachhuber, 'The Absoluteness of Christianity and Relativity of All History: Two Strands in Ferdinand Christian Baur's Thought,' in *Ferdinand Christian Baur*, ed. Bauspiess, Landmesser, and Lincicum, pp. 330-1.

sons' (Gal. 4:4-5; that's salvation). Populism as this book defines it is a promising framework for theologically rich exegesis and exposition of the Bible, a noble aim of biblical theology of either and both Testaments.

2.4 Recovering an Ecology of Man

A fourth reason for hope for a populist approach to Scripture, Christian faith, and lived-out life is its viability in the current international crisis facing us in view of humanity, sexuality, gender, the family, and related issues. A 2015 statement called the Salzburg Declaration[26] issued in Austria has received little press in the English-speaking world. It deserves to be better known. Entitled, in English, 'Current Threats to Human Creatureliness and Their Overcoming: Life According to the Creator's Will,' the statement was issued by the Internationale Konferenz Bekennender Gemeinschaften (International Conference of Confessing Congregations), a title that echoes the church coalition that opposed Hitler.

The statement affirms, 'The "ecology of man" means that humans are to treat their own nature (and not only the nature that surrounds them) with care, respecting the order of creation and the commandments that God has given them to their own benefit.' It sets forth 'the biblical witness as the basis for an "ecology of man".' It identifies 'present attacks on man as God's creation with special reference to gender theory,' with particular reference to Judith Butler and her influence in elite thought and international governmental social policy. It details 'the need for a new reflection on the biblical revelation as a precondition for an "ecology of man".'

The Salzburg conferees were German-speaking scholars and church leaders representing Roman Catholic, Eastern Orthodox, mainline Protestant, and evangelical churches in western and eastern Europe. That coalition in itself is unusual. But even more striking is the biblical realism informing the entire statement. Genesis 1–3 and the Ten Commandments and the teachings of Jesus and the apostles are all deployed as binding norms for Christian thought in this critical domain in our time of unprecedented crisis. It is unprecedented if for no other reason than that we move daily into the uncharted waters of an international holocaust of aborted babies, with about 1.5 *billion* killed worldwide just since 1980, among them over eighteen million African

---

26. http://www.ikbg.net/, accessed 20 May 2019.

American babies in the U.S. alone since 1973.[27] The human poverty – personal, social, economic, political – of such statistics is staggering, and all the more so in light of God's love for the life He creates (including in the womb; Psalms 71:6; 127:3; 139:13) and determination to hold accountable those who devalue such life.

Moreover, the primary author of the Salzburg Declaration is Werner Neuer, an evangelical theologian who has led the way in rediscovering Adolf Schlatter's importance and who is a strong proponent of biblical authority and the Bible's view of sexuality. Some may recall that he authored a book *Man and Woman in Christian Perspective*, translated by Gordon Wenham and published by Crossway in 1991. It was one of the earlier substantive entries in the egalitarian-complementarian debate. It drew not only on Scripture but on social scientific literature of the time. It came down squarely on the traditionalist side. Now a quarter century later this same author with strong collegial support is representing the historic consensual Christian outlook on human flourishing based on the Bible in an international ecumenical declaration.

Throughout the declaration, reference is made to the complicity of elitist Protestant churches in gender theory, abortion, and other views and activities declared sinful in the Bible. Here is the problem, quoting the Declaration:

> All the above-mentioned Biblical beliefs of the Christian Churches have been held in common by all Christians (in the sense of a *magnus consensus*) well into the 20th century, despite doctrinal differences by Catholics, Protestants and Orthodox. They have likewise found confirmation within the pre and extra-Christian natural law tradition. This common witness is now under threat as never before, particularly under the influence of certain Protestants groups which, under the influence of the Zeitgeist, have abandoned this common witness and hence deepened the existing divisions among the Churches. Not only is the ecumenical unity [a]ffected among the Churches, but also the internal unity within the different Churches. With respect to the witness of the Biblical account of creation there is now a painful split throughout the Churches of Europe and North America. This makes a common witness of Christians and the Churches in the face of secular culture and non-Christian religions less and less possible.

27. http://www.numberofabortions.com/, accessed 20 May 2019.

But a common witness is possible based on the populist convictions of the emerging world church, which turn out to be the biblical convictions of a continuing core of highly trained mainline European church leaders who have not abandoned the historic faith and its belief in a sacred Scripture with life-preserving truth for the human race at present.

2.5 (Re-) Connection with the Ecumenical Christian Heritage of Biblical Inerrancy

A fifth reason for hope for a populist approach to Scripture, Christian faith, and lived-out life is the view of Scripture held not only by populist believers, which is generally a high view, but by more than half of the Christians on planet earth. I speak of the Roman Catholic communion, to which over half of the world Christian population belongs. Protestants are about half that, and evangelicals only a percentage of Protestants. What the majority of Christians in world history are taught about the Bible is surely of interest to a numeric subgroup like ourselves, especially if their view were to happen to support our own.

I am not here affirming Roman Catholic ecclesiology or soteriology; I side with Luther and Calvin and the Protestant heritage in their biblical critique of Catholicism. At the same time we must note that the official Roman Catholic view of Scripture is just as inerrantist as the Chicago Statement and more theologically grounded.[28] If international church unity matters, now and in the future, we are going in the wrong direction if we hallow as primary discussion partners the elite movement which at the Enlightenment departed not only from the Protestant Scholastic view of Scripture but also from the historic consensual view on display, e.g., in Augustine and upheld in an unbroken chain to this hour by many (though by no means all) Roman Catholic scholars and official church teaching.

Church historian John Woodbridge, probably evangelicalism's leading authority on the history of inerrantist thought, reminded me in personal conversation recently of the high regard B. B. Warfield and J. Gresham

---

28. See Pablo T. Gadenz, 'Magisterial Teaching on the Inspiration and Truth of Scripture: Precedents and Prospects,' *Letter & Spirit* 6 (2010): pp. 67-91, commended by Jeffrey L. Morrow in his review of Eckart Schmidt, '... *das Wort Gottes immer mehr zu lieben*': *Joseph Ratzingers Bibelhermeneutik im Kontext der Exegesegeschichte der römisch-katholischen Kirche*, http://www.bookreviews.org/bookdetail.asp?TitleId=10523. In *RBL* 02/2018, accessed February 19, 2018.

Machen had for the Roman Catholic doctrine of Scripture, which they wholeheartedly affirmed.[29] Pope Benedict XVI, known as Cardinal Ratzinger when he was the doctrinal overseer of the Catholic church, wrote extensively against elitist hermeneutics and in some ways defied it in his three volume series called *Jesus of Nazareth*.[30] He also supported the Catholic church's inerrantist view of Scripture, refining it only by making more explicit the sense in which the written Word leads to the living Word Jesus Christ. I think he may overstate here with this Barthian accent, and I refer you to an excellent study on this by Matthew Barrett at Midwestern Seminary: 'Is Our Doctrine of Inerrancy Christological Enough? The Future of Inerrancy and the Necessity of Dogmatics.'[31] Barrett shows that Christ the Word calls us to full loyalty to Him *and* to Scripture, not to Him and not so much if at all to Scripture as Barth argued.

The point is that the worldwide Christian resurgence outside the formerly Christian West, which I am calling populist, with its tendency toward the view that the totality of Scripture is totally true, finds an ally in the world's largest Christian confession. Christians everywhere should affirm this important plot of common ground. Protestants do well to regard Catholics not as enemies but as allies when it comes to the doctrine of Scripture's truth and should pray for our collective witness to biblical authority, the true gospel of Christ, and the living Lordship of Christ in the face of opposition and persecution from post- and anti-Christian ideologies from whatever quarters.

2.6 Gospel Impetus from Populism's Daughters and Sons Coming of Age

A sixth reason for hope for a populist approach to Scripture, Christian faith, and lived-out life is that it is already with us bearing fruit in significant strength and numbers in the post-Christian West.

---

29. On Machen's high regard for Roman Catholic teaching on Scripture, see also John Woodbridge, 'The Fundamentalist-Modernist Controversy,' in *Evangelical Scholarship, Retrospects and Prospects*, eds. Dirk R. Buursma, Katya Covrett, and Verlyn D. Verbrugge, festschrift for Stanley N. Gundry (Grand Rapids: Zondervan, 2017), p. 106.

30. Vol. 1 (2007): *Jesus of Nazareth: From the Baptism in the Jordan to the Transfiguration*; vol. 2 (2011): *Jesus of Nazareth: Holy Week: From the Entrance Into Jerusalem to The Resurrection*; vol. 3 (2012): *Jesus of Nazareth: The Infancy Narratives*.

31. *Presbyterion* 44 (Spring 2018) pp. 25-41.

Immigrant believers and churches in many of our cities and elsewhere are creating a fresh Christian presence. In St Louis, Missouri, U.S.A., near the location of the seminary where I teach, there is a Nepalese, a Congolese, a Sudanese, and a pan-African presence, along with Korean and Chinese churches more numerous. I'm sure there are others. One of my students is starting a Brazilian fellowship. The Bible is hallowed among these groups, not doubted. Perhaps they can re-evangelize us North American pagans with our animist idolatry and folk religious syncretism that conflates American with Christian, adding in European conviction that autonomous rational criticism of God's Word somehow honors Him.

Or look at the academy. I do not have hard numbers. But when I was at Trinity Evangelical Divinity School near Chicago, our academic dean was Tite Tiénou from Ivory Coast, Africa. One New Testament colleague was from Hong Kong and came to us after a PhD at Harvard. Another was from Singapore with a PhD from Emory. At Beeson Divinity School there is a young New Testament scholar with an Aberdeen PhD from the Dominican Republic. At Beeson there is another New Testament scholar with an Aberdeen PhD born in South Korea. She is Dr Sydney Park. You can read her testimony in the book she co-wrote with Old Testament scholar Kenneth A. Mathews, *The Post-Racial Church: A Biblical Framework for Multiethnic Reconciliation*.[32] It is appended to this book.

Despite the racism Park faced as a girl in Chicago city and suburban schools, and despite hardened unbelief in college at the University of Chicago, God united her in faith in Christ with many millions of other Koreans in our times. Like the other scholars I have mentioned and their peers all around the world, she went from racial minority, in this country, to a Christian scholar and treasured seminary professor. Her *A Biblical Theology of Women*[33] is slated to be published by T & T Clark in coming months.

Since 2014 I and a pastoral colleague work twice annually with a man of color in Cape Town, South Africa, who rose from a racially disadvantaged location under Apartheid to acquire an advanced

---

32. Grand Rapids: Kregel, 2011. See pp. 266-70.
33. London: T & T Clark, 2019.

degree at Stellenbosch. He now teaches hundreds of bright but educationally disadvantaged pastors in the Cape Flats. They are not plotting political insurrection or reading liberation theology but poring over Scripture, Spurgeon, the Reformers, and other greats of the Christian tradition. And they are preaching Christ crucified and risen in neighborhoods that are poverty-haunted and gang-ridden, seeing many baptisms and enlisting men and women in lives of discipleship. They are preaching and teaching in the region's bleak prisons. The man I work with left the Baptist Union there because of its elitist liberalism, a problem with many Baptist churches worldwide who have lost faith in the Book.

I am just scratching the surface. My point is that we do see erosion in Western evangelical scholarship with people like David Congdon and Bart Ehrman becoming elitist cheerleaders, and evangelical scholars distancing themselves from biblical authority when it comes to various issues. But there is significant movement in the opposite direction going on right under our noses. A man I taught in Romania when he was a college student in the 1990s and who grew up under Romanian Communist persecution has become a full professor of theology at Gordon Conwell Theological Seminary.[34] The president of Károli Gáspár University in Budapest, Hungary, Prof. Dr Peter Balla, likewise weathered Communist oppression in his younger years but persevered to write both a doctoral dissertation[35] and the subsequent scholarly publication that follows in the German academic tradition, the *Habilitation*.[36] They, other scholars I have mentioned in this section, and many others have a doctrinal and biblical foundation forged in the fires of first- and second-generation Christianity under social ostracism and sometimes persecution. They represent fresh means of grace in Western regions like ours that have lost faith in Scripture and seem to fear the censure of the elite more than God's verdict on their loyalties and publications.

34. Reference here is to Dr Adonis Vidu: see https://www.gordonconwell.edu/academics/view-faculty-member.cfm?faculty_id=57851&grp_id=8947, accessed January 30, 2019.

35. Peter Balla, *Challenges to New Testament Theology: An Attempt to Justify the Enterprise* (Tübingen: J. C. B. Mohr, 1997). This was a University of Edinburgh doctoral thesis.

36. Peter Balla, *The Child-Parent Relationship in the New Testament and Its Environment* (Tübingen: Mohr Siebeck, 2003). This was his second doctoral thesis at the Evangelical Lutheran Theological University, Budapest, Hungary.

3. Conclusion: Two Testimonies

What *is* God's verdict on the tension I have highlighted in these lectures? Ulrich Wilckens, whose insight into elitist inadequacy is so important, calls repeatedly for a return to God in scholarship. But how? Wilckens also calls for a rediscovery of love. The exhortation is well-taken. But his counsel seems to be primarily: fight harder against those in error like Barth did against his liberal forebears in the 1920s,[37] though many think Barth ended up losing touch with God, too.[38] Wilckens' diagnosis of historical-criticism's ills is more effective than his prescription for a cure.

But I do not fault him, because I have no tidy final answers, either. But I will make this prediction. If elitist misdirection is in the future overcome, diminished, or perhaps even redeemed, it will come by God's direct action in individual hearts – not only that, but not without that. Recalling the (Baptist) revivalist tradition in which Christ's death for my sins and resurrection life became real to me, and in which my wife (a former Roman Catholic) was led to affirm a similar personal commitment during the first of our now forty-five years of marriage, I am well aware how God calls sinners to Christ. Therefore He could come to our aid even at this present time too. I offer a pair of testimonies that may encourage hope, resolve, and – why not? – worship.

In 2015 Wilckens (born 1928 in Hamburg, Germany) told an interviewer for the German Christian magazine *ideaSpektrum* this:[39]

> I'll explain to you how I became a Christian. Growing up there was no praying in our house. My father was a staff doctor in the military and 100 per cent convinced there is no God. And so I also believed in nothing. In January 1945, so shortly before WWII ended, I was drafted as a 16 year old. We received six weeks of training. Then we were thrown into the war near Munich. We were supposed to stop the American 6th Armored Division with small arms and grenade launchers. I was dug in 100 yards in advance of the front. I heard the rumble of 200 advancing tanks. I will never forget the terrifying sound. I was in fear of death. A schoolgirl friend had given me a pocket NT. I pulled it out and read, 'in the world you have tribulation ... but be of good cheer: I have overcome the world' (John 16:33 NASB & ESV).

---

37. Wilckens, *Historische Kritik der historich-kritischen Exegese*, e.g., p. 384.

38. Some will not find the story told here reassuring: Christiane Tietz, 'Karl Barth and Charlotte von Kirschbaum,' *Theology Today* 74/2 (2017) pp. 86-111.

39. *ideaSpektrum* 14 (2015), p. 21.

I did not only read these lines: I heard them. You asked me how someone hears the voice of God today. These words for me were not just something I read out of a tattered Bible: it was God addressing me. This voice of Jesus Christ – it stuck with me my whole life.

ideaSpektrum: How did you survive the tank attack?

Wilckens: It was frightful! For decades I could not talk about it. It was a bloodbath. Most of my comrades lay dead on the ground. A junior officer gathered the remains. That I came out of it in one piece I attribute to God's voice that I heard.

ideaSpektrum: You found your way to Christian faith through the war. Others lost theirs through the war.

Wilckens: Every man must regard events for himself. I cannot compare my experience with that of another. But when I tell what I went through, there are very many people who listen attentively, because they hear something genuine.

The entire interview with Wilckens is printed as an appendix to this book and is well worth digesting. But even the bit reproduced above justifies the question: might true Christian testimony still be so genuine that it could challenge even in elitist circles what Lamin Sanneh calls 'the allergy of a secular West to any suggestion of a return to Christianity'?[40] History is replete with stories of those indifferent or opposed to Christianity finding themselves drawn to it, whether Augustine the refined intellectual, John Newton the wicked slave trader, or the late Nabeel Qureshi, former Muslim apologist whose witness lives on in the important publication of two major books.[41]

Here is a second testimony, this one from InterVarsity publisher Andy Le Peu on the occasion of author Jim Sire's death. Le Peu calls Sire 'a keystone in the intellectual renewal of [North American] evangelicalism'.[42] Le Peu tells this story:

The two of us were at a large dinner held in honor of John W. Alexander, the recently retired president of InterVarsity Christian Fellowship. At the

---

40. Sanneh, *Whose Religion Is Christianity?*, p. 83.

41. I.e., *Seeking Allah, Finding Jesus: A Devout Muslim Encounters Christianity*, expanded edition (Grand Rapids: Zondervan, 2016); *No God But One: Allah or Jesus? A Former Muslim Investigates the Evidence for Islam and Christianity* (Grand Rapids: Zondervan, 2016).

42. Accessed at http://andyunedited.ivpress.com/2018/02/james_w_sire_1933-2018.php, Feb. 3, 2019.

dinner, probably held in 1985, Dr Alexander exhorted the group to not become too enamored with ideas about Christianity, its philosophical underpinnings, its intellectual implications. Yes, they had their place in apologetics and so forth, but these ideas were not the center of Christianity. Christ was. We should always and ever focus on Jesus. The person of Jesus is and should be our center.

As I sat next to Jim, I wondered what he would think of this as someone who had spent a career focused on the very kinds of ideas Alexander was saying were of secondary importance. After it was over, Jim turned to me and said, 'You know, he's right. Jesus is the center.'

I was surprised if not stunned. And from that point on I noticed a marked shift in Jim's own writing and his own spiritual life. In retrospect I see the humility of someone with substantial intellectual accomplishments, someone who was willing to remain open to the Spirit and to grow throughout life. That is perhaps the most important lesson he taught.

The worldwide populist church calls us, as does the late James Sire's example, to humility regarding any intellectual accomplishments, to open-ness to the Spirit, to lifelong growth in grace and knowledge, and might I add to more reverence for the Bible than for criticism of it.

For as Lamin Sanneh states, 'A post-Christian West is not so far gone that it cannot make live contact with a post-Western Christianity.'[43]

---

43. Sanneh, *Whose Religion Is Christianity?*, p. 80. For a description of how that might take place and in fact is happening, see Jerry Trousdale and Glenn Sunshine with Gregory C. Benoit, *The Kingdom Unleashed: How Jesus' 1st-Century Kingdom Values Are Transforming Thousands of Cultures and Awakening His Church* (Murfreesboro, TN: DMM Library, 2018).

Testimony of a German Lutheran Bishop and New Testament Scholar: 'Easter is the central theme of my life'[1]

He is one of the most unusual Protestant theology professors in German-speaking Europe: Ulrich Wilckens (Lübeck). During his time as theology professor and bishop he was by no means regarded as a pious advocate of confessional Christianity. That all changed after a near-death experience. Against expectations, he recovered. Since then he is among the most outspoken churchmen in Germany. idea *reporter Karsten Huhn talked with him.*

idea: Herr Bishop, by now you have celebrated Easter many times. Do you really still celebrate this occasion?

Wilckens: Absolutely! Easter is the central theme of my life. If Christ was not resurrected, I would have to say with Paul: my faith is in vain (1 Cor. 15:14). In the cross and resurrection of Christ God in His sovereignty works our redemption. In this certainty I live.

idea: That Christ rose – everyone says that.

Wilckens: Unfortunately not everyone says that any more, but actually very few.

idea: What makes you so sure that there is something real to the resurrection?

Wilckens: To start with, my historical-exegetical work. In addition: the ongoing experience within myself that the living Christ is at work.

---

1. A translation of the interview found at http://kath.net/news/50015. ©First published in *ideaSpektrum* 14/2015. Used by permission. Translation by R. Yarbrough.

Reason is a Gift of God

idea: That conviction was not so easy for the author and Enlightenment figure Gotthold Ephraim Lessing (1729–1781). He charged that the truths of the Bible could not be verified: 'That is the ugly wide ditch over which I could not pass, however often and earnestly I attempted the leap.'

Wilckens: That view is advocated at present by many theologians, recently by New Testament scholar Ulrich Luz who teaches in Switzerland. But they reflect too little on what presuppositions are informing their judgment. They see it as reason, which *a priori* exerts control over the possibilities of God's action. Here the decisive criterion is human experience, concealed behind the veil of so-called science.

idea: They have good reason for this: reason is the most important instrument of a scientist – and of theologians too.

Wilckens: But reason is not some entity complete in itself. It can rather arrive at widely varying results. There is 'reason' that reverences God and reckons with His reality. That is the presupposition of all knowing. In this understanding reason is based ultimately and emphatically not in the experience of human science but in the experience that God exists and is at work. I do not attribute my reason and capacity to know something to myself; this is rather a gift and task of God.

The Problem of Contemporary Theology

idea: One of the dominant Enlightenment theologians was Ernst Troeltsch (1865–1923). In view of fading certainties for faith in Life of Jesus studies, he decided, 'Everything is tottering.' Nothing is for sure in theology any more.

Wilckens: With this statement he underscored the uncertainty that reigns in current theology to this day. Whoever explains the faith of the New Testament as growing out of the ancient religions, therefore as not rooted in God, but invented by man, has nothing more to do with the Christian faith. Many theologians no longer believe in God Himself in His actual effects; they rather cast faith in God as religious sentiment. For them, the resurrection is a religious feeling that arises in man: in the end everything will turn out OK.

The Resurrection is Based on Fact

idea: Can the resurrection be based on facts?

Wilckens: Yes, I think so. I think the New Testament reports need to be taken seriously as history. Take the empty tomb. Many scholars think that Jesus' empty tomb is an invention. I think that is totally unrealistic. At that time anyone in Jerusalem could check whether the tomb was occupied or not. Moreover, there was a lively discussion between Jews and Christians whether Jesus' disciples stole His corpse (Matt. 28:11-15). That is indirect admission that the body was no longer in the grave.

idea: An empty tomb by itself is not yet a resurrection, however.

Wilckens: In addition, women at the empty tomb learned from an angel that God raised Jesus. In those days people were familiar with visions and audial encounters with God, hearing and seeing His reality. Just before this the women were deeply troubled, and Jesus' disciples after His death were on the verge of abandoning their faith in Him, returning to their native Galilee – they could take no solace in the prospect that He would resurrect. For in Jewish teaching it was excluded that someone could rise from the dead prior to the end of all things. How would the first Christians – who were all Jews – come up with this outrageous idea on their own? Today many view that as plausible, but in the thought of the time it was a shocking notion.

Becoming a Christian in the Trenches

idea: If someone claimed today to stand at an empty grave and to hear God's voice, for many that would be a case for psychiatry.

Wilckens: We hear the voice of God today, just in other ways. Let me explain to you how I became a Christian. Growing up there was no praying in our house. My father was a staff doctor in the military and 100 per cent convinced there is no God. And so I also believed in nothing. In January 1945, so shortly before WWII ended, I was drafted as a 16 year old. We received six weeks of training. Then we were thrown into the war near Munich. We were supposed to stop the American 6th Armored Division with small arms and grenade launchers. I was dug in 100 yards in advance of the front. I heard the rumble of 200 advancing tanks. I will never forget the terrifying sound. I was in fear of death. A schoolgirl friend had given me a pocket New Testament. I pulled it out and read, 'In the world you have tribulation ...'

idea: '... *but be of good cheer: I have overcome the world*' (John 16:33 KJV).

Wilckens: I did not only read these lines: I heard them. You asked me how someone hears the voice of God today. These words for me were not just something I read out of a tattered Bible: it was God addressing me. This voice of Jesus Christ – it stuck with me my whole life.

idea: How did you survive the tank attack?

Wilckens: It was frightful! For decades I could not talk about it. It was a bloodbath. Most of my comrades lay dead on the ground. A junior officer gathered the remains. That I came out of it in one piece I trace back to God's voice that I heard.

idea: You found your way to Christian faith through the war. Others lost theirs through the war.

Wilckens: Every man must regard events for himself. I cannot compare my experience with that of another. But when I tell what I went through, there are very many people who listen attentively, because they hear something genuine.

I Debated with Marxists

idea: After the war you studied theology in Heidelberg and Tübingen. The competition between the two faculties is legendary. How do they differ?

Wilckens: Tübingen is smaller and full of Pietists speaking Schwabian dialect. I recall in particular Ernst Fuchs (1903–1983). He was a typical Schwabian. He fascinated me, a northern German, no end. I could barely understand him, his dialect was so thick. When he interpreted the Bible, he basically always explained what it meant to him – but I did not understand that until later.

idea: You finished your *Habilitation* [second doctoral dissertation] and were called to Marburg, and then later to Berlin and Hamburg.

Wilckens: I arrived in Berlin in the middle of the student demonstrations [of the late 1960s]. Deep into the night I disputed with Marxists and Leninists. I was pushed to my limits to keep up with them intellectually.

idea: Were you able to convince the disciples of Marx and Mao?

Wilckens: No, but perhaps I was able to make them think. Every fortnight my wife and I invited students for supper. Afterward there would be a conversational slugfest. Eventually we broke for a midnight snack. Then discussions became more personal. The atmosphere altered. The strident revolutionaries became almost wistful. I observed that behind the gruff exterior, there had to be hiding a deep yearning for a sure ultimate homeland.

The Church Needs a Foundational Renewal

idea: From 1981–91 you were the bishop of the diocese of Holstein-Lübeck. At that time you complained, 'The substance of the faith is evaporating. More and more people know nothing of the Christian faith. It gains no traction in their own life, nor do they want it to. Such perceptions of the practical irrelevance of the Christian faith reach deep into the membership of our church.'

Wilckens: This is the way things are still – except things have grown even worse. At that time I observed that not only theology students were running aground in the faith but also members of the church leadership. When I mentioned angels in an annual report, the synod laughed me to scorn, because they regarded the existence of angels as nonsense.

idea: Recently the *Frankfurter Allgemeine Zeitung* [the *New York Times* of Germany] reported, 'The German Protestant Church Is Not Shrinking: It Is Imploding.'

Wilckens: Such observations are proof that the church needs a fundamental renewal. We cannot celebrate the Reformation anniversary in 2017: we need to let ourselves be reformed! All devout groups that up till now have been tending their own garden must work together for this. Then it would be clear that there are a lot more God-fearing people than is publicly acknowledged. If only everyone would work together!

The Day for Christ and a Church Convention without a Witness to the Faith

idea: Who could pull together such a gathering?

Wilckens: An example would be the 'Day for Christ' last year in Stuttgart.

idea: That's happening again this year.

Wilckens: Yes, but unfortunately it coincides with the Protestant Church Convention! That means the 'Day for Christ' will not be free to bring about spiritual renewal.

idea: Why not?

Wilckens: The Protestant Church Convention is a secular media event, intentionally so.

idea: The Church Convention is a rally of robustly joyful Christian people.

Wilckens: Robustly joyful people – yes! Many young people – wonderful! But how important is the Christian faith there? The devotionals, sermons, and theological lectures deal with everything imaginable – but they don't touch on the center of the faith.

idea: Not even you, as a bishop, were able to stop the decline of the church.

Wilckens: That is correct. In retrospect I tell myself: I should have done more. For example, I should have had a stronger hand in the training of pastoral candidates. Perhaps in that way I could have influenced, not the trainers, but the future pastors themselves. Back then it already required courage for someone to testify to their faith in Jesus Christ and to take the Bible seriously as Holy Scripture. Pastoral trainees all came from university programs where their professors had already talked them out of such convictions. I'm afraid that I didn't speak up enough about this but just mentioned it casually.

Rarely Encountered Such Spiteful People

idea: Were you an unsuccessful bishop?

Wilckens: I can answer with neither yes nor no. What was astonishing, though, was the success of a plea to all church executive boards to begin every meeting with reflection on a biblical text and then prayer for the renewal of the church. More than half of all congregations registered positive feedback on this. On the other hand, I became the target of the animosity of virulent feminist theologians. Rarely have I ever encountered such spiteful people. At first I did not take their attacks seriously. In the end, my wife is also a theologian – without however being a feminist.

New Life Was Given to Me

idea: Were you happy when you stepped down from ten years in the bishop's office?

Wilckens: No, I wanted to stand for election again, but suddenly I became deathly ill. I was diagnosed with pancreatic cancer, which as a rule leads to death. The doctors gave me six months. I endured a nine-hour surgery. To my amazed and great joy I did not die but became healthy again. New life was given to me.

idea: You used the time to write a theology of the New Testament in six volumes. Your fellow professors gave you the silent treatment. There are hardly any reviews of these books.

Wilckens: Unfortunately that is the truth.

idea: Your theology has fallen out of fashion. Do you have an explanation?

Wilckens: We're dealing with no less than a captivity to radically critical, liberal thought, what we might call the 'ugly wide ditch' into which many have fallen in the wake of the Enlightenment and of the demythologization of the Bible by Rudolf Bultmann (1884–1976). This theology bears atheistic features and continues to spread. I made this development the theme of my recent book *Kritik der Bibelkritik*. My impression is that many theologians feel it is unnecessary even to engage my arguments.

idea: At what point has theology gone off the rails?

Wilckens: Since the Enlightenment, faith has been widely understood as something concocted in man – as subjective religiosity. The sense of God being an active presence in and party to faith has vanished. For that reason, theology, like the church, needs a deep renewal. We need fresh discovery of the reality of God.

No Anxiety about Death, Because There Is Resurrection

idea: Mr Wilckens, before our appointment you told me that it might take a while for you to open the door after I rang the doorbell.

Wilckens: Last year I took a bad fall. It was the only day of the winter when the streets were icy and slick. I realized it too late. I totally wrecked my right shoulder, and add to that a fractured pelvis. Then at the clinic I suffered a stroke. For weeks I lay in the neurology ward. Then I was transferred to rehab, though no one thought rehab would be possible. But I could finally be released and return home. My physical therapist trained me to attain independence once more. In the meantime, my wife had to go into a nursing home. I visit her there every other day.

idea: You are on the home stretch of your life.

Wilckens: So it is.

idea: Is that an unsettling thought for you?

Wilckens: No, but it can be good that that's what lies ahead. No one knows what tomorrow will bring. I place my life in God's hands every evening – let Him do with me what pleases Him. And however painful the road ahead: there is the resurrection! That is where my hope lies.

idea: Many thanks for the discussion!

Ulrich Wilckens (86 at the time of this interview) was bishop of the Holstein-Lübeck district of the Nordelbische Church from 1981-1991. Prior to that he served as Professor of New Testament in Marburg, Berlin, and Hamburg. He is author of the six-volume Theology of the New Testament. *Chronicling his shift in outlook are particularly the books* Kritik der Bibelkritik *(2012) and* Historische Kritik der historisch-kritischen Exegese: Von der Aufklärung bis zur Gegenwart (2017). *Wilckens is married and the father of three daughters.*

The Cross and Human Healing

Dr M. Sydney Park, New Testament professor at Beeson Divinity School in Birmingham, Alabama, wrote the paragraphs below in chapter ten of a book she co-authored with Old Testament scholar Kenneth A. Mathews, *The Post-Racial Church: A Biblical Framework for Multiethnic Reconciliation* (Grand Rapids: Kregel, 2011), pp. 266-70. This excerpt from their book appears below with their permission.

Dr Park's pilgrimage in important respects mirrors the experiences that early Christians worked through on their way to the kind of mixed-heritage congregations like the one that grew up in Syrian Antioch (where people were first called Christians: Acts 11:26) and gradually replicated across the Roman Empire.

One of the major implications of Acts (and later Eph. 2–3) is that through the gospel message the *echthra* (hostility; see Gen. 3:15 LXX; Eph. 2:14, 16) between peoples is replaced by solidarity – even love – because of Christ. Acts ends with that message still going forth.

We are in the same salvation-historical position today, except that the implications of human hostility and the price tag of regional and international inability to come together for the common good and God's glory is a starker reality than ever. Dr Park points a way for hearts to be changed so that people might be more inclined to value others rather than primarily themselves.

A TESTIMONY OF CONVERSION AND HOPE
Dr Sydney Park

Racism Begets Racism

I (Park) was not always a Christian. Although I grew up in a Christian home, attending church every Sunday (Presbyterian), I proclaimed myself an atheist in college and only came to faith in January of 1987, a year and a half after college graduation. My conversion was different from many 'coming to faith' stories I've heard through the years. I came to confess Jesus Christ as my Savior after thinking about the process of photosynthesis and ecology, which ultimately led to a reconsideration of creation and evolution. The entire process took approximately four hours on one cold January afternoon in my apartment in Evanston, Illinois. But this story is not simply about my conversion from atheism to Christianity. It is a story of how the Christian faith eventually affected my perspective on people outside of my own racial heritage, Korean. When I was eight years old, I immigrated to the United States with my family in 1971. As I attended public schools in the city of Chicago, I quickly learned that I was a 'Chink.' The school playground is not always a setting for innocent play, but oftentimes the platform for cruelty and malice. Racial slurs such as 'flat-face,' 'moon-face,' 'slanty-eyes' were droned into my ears on a daily basis. Name calling and various demeaning gestures (drawing out the eyelids to make slants, the 'ah-so's', etc.) usually led to physical jostling and sometimes blows. I soon learned that in order to cope with the daily onslaught of racial prejudice, I needed to develop my own arsenal of racial insults.

After a couple of years in the inner-city of Chicago, we moved to the suburbs, Glen Ellyn, Illinois. My parents were convinced that the move to the suburbs would diminish playground disasters and most definitely improve my language. They were right to assume that suburbia would offer a more genteel class of people, but they were entirely wrong if they had expected less racism as a byproduct of higher economic status. Yes, the playground brawls ceased, but racism was practiced on a whole new level. When I was a high school freshman in 1974, there were four Asian families, three Black families and one Indian family in our school district. And the minorities were subtly but firmly rejected from the popular cliques. Without any physical violence or even verbal insults, I felt racism envelop me from every direction. Now it was hushed whispers every time I approached and the burst of laughter and giggles each time I passed by. It was the unsmiling stares that made me feel not different, but *alien*. It was the silent unfriendly stare from the grocery store clerk who had just greeted the previous white customer with ease and friendliness. I knew that I was different and an object of ridicule in the city; in the suburbs, I learned that I would never be accepted as an equal. As a teenage girl going through adolescent identity issues, living in the suburbs convinced me that unless I looked 'white' I would never be pretty.

But college changed everything. I was surrounded not only by numerous Asians, but also Jews (in 1977 at University of Chicago, there were only a few Hispanic and Black students). I found friends who understood racism through personal experience. And this solidarity as victims of racism gave strength and courage to our reverse racism against the Whites. After all, the Whites were the primary source of my experience with racism. But as I had learned in high school and college history courses, they were also the oppressors for Jews and Blacks. Why shouldn't I treat them with equal hatred and racism? But as I progressed in college, I experienced racism from an entirely different group – African-Americans. University of Chicago is located in Hyde Park, a neighborhood classified as the 'ghetto' comprised predominantly by Blacks. Anytime I walked through these neighborhoods, I was greeted with racial slurs and gestures now all too familiar. I was the object of ridicule for not only Whites, but also Blacks. I began to develop a deep-seated anger and resentment towards all races apart from my own. I was suspicious of all races, expected racism everywhere and racial profiling was on auto-pilot in my mind. And I did not seek ways to 'get along' but life was now about the Hobbesian ethos, 'survival of the fittest.'

'One of Us?'

I wish I could say that after I became a Christian my experience of racism stopped – it didn't. When I was attending Southwestern Baptist Theological Seminary in Fort Worth, Texas, I was indeed a 'foreigner' to the Southerners (yes, the school is more accurately in the Southwest, but it attracted students from many Southern states). I was not only a Yankee, but an 'oriental.' But what made things more interesting was that I had developed a southern drawl during my stay in Texas. A student once confessed to my white friend: 'She dresses like us, she talks like us, but she doesn't look like us! I'm so confused!' Even when I had removed the differences as much as possible, I was still 'not the same' simply on the virtue of my ethnicity. Of course, the accent didn't help – it just confused people even more. Once, when I was driving from Houston to Fort Worth, I lost my sense of direction and couldn't find Interstate 45. So, as I was making a U-turn in one of the streets, I noticed a man walking by and I stopped to ask for directions. After I asked for directions, the man scratched his head and said: 'Honey, is your daddy white?' No matter how 'American' I became people would always ask: 'Where are you from?' meaning, 'Where are your people from?' But racism or discomfort with ethnic difference was not only particular to the South or even North America. When I was in Aberdeen, Scotland in 2001-2004, I encountered the forms of mockery (giggling, the gesture with the eyes and blatant racial slurs) I had not experienced since the days of high school and college. And I can't imagine that racism in various forms will cease in this world.

The Cross: The Healing Balm for Racism

If I continued to be the victim of racism in various degrees after I became a Christian, then what is the 'conversion' story? It is not the world, nor how the world views me or treats me that have changed, but how *I* changed through the process of knowing Christ. As significant as my conversion from atheism to Christianity was, my conversion was thorough-going on several levels. Although it took time, through the years of being a disciple of Christ, I discovered I no longer had reason to practice racism. My initial reason for racism may have been simply retaliation, but the deeper motive went beyond 'getting back at them.' The effects of racism filtered down to the deepest level of my psyche and made me feel less than human. I was never 'good enough' and I would never be 'enough.' I was perpetually second class in the eyes of the majority; always the 'foreigner' although I've been a naturalized U.S. citizen since 1977 and speak perfect English. The incentive for lashing out against the other races was the impact racism had on my self-esteem. This profound need for worth was met through Jesus Christ.

That the Son of God hung on the cross to save me from inveterate sin supplied me with all the self-esteem I needed. There is no greater statement on the worthiness of human life as God's creation than the cross. God as Creator made me fully human and God the Redeemer made me fully reconciled. When I was at Trinity Evangelical Divinity School in 1999–2000, I remember a small group session where each student shared what served as an encouragement and motivation for them on any given day. Some said that kind words from people were encouraging, others confessed that love of their family (wives, children, parents) supplied the needed strength, and still others pointed to the simple beauty of God's creation reflected in nature as uplifting elements in their lives. And I realized, at this point that there was only one thing that truly gave me hope and encouragement with respect to my self-esteem. It was not the kind words of friends, for I was sure that my friends not only sought to see me in the best possible light, but I was certain that they did not truly 'know me' in all my sin. It was not even the love of my family, since I could not imagine my parents not loving me in spite of my flaws. In the Asian culture, the chance that parents would not love their children is about as good as an orange tree bearing apples. '*Of course*, my parents love me! Isn't it obligatory?' The only thing that truly encouraged me was Jesus Christ on the cross. Given God's holiness and righteousness, he is in no way obligated to love me, yet he does. Given God's omniscience, he sees my sins more clearly than I can admit them to myself, yet he does not turn away, but hangs on the cross. God sees me as I am in my frailty and failure. He sees me in my desperation to be loved and provides his profound love willingly and eternally. Beauty of the world will pass, friends will come and go and even my family may reject me, but God's love as seen in the cross endures forever.

With respect to other races, there is no more enmity, there is no more striving for approval, there is now peace (Eph. 2:11-16). I have no more reason to approach other races with suspicion, anger and resentment and I have no need to accuse. Whatever race I encounter now, it is an occasion for testimony to the goodness of God through his Son Jesus Christ (1 Cor. 9:19-23). Regardless of race, all Christians are now my 'kin' and I call people not of my own race 'my brothers and sisters.' And I find that the most genuine and penetrating relationships I have are with people with the same abiding love for Christ, regardless of race or ethnicity. My world has most certainly changed from anger and resentment to peace. But, it has also been transformed from one ethnicity to multiethnic diversity. And even more, it is not merely the North Americans, but the Scottish and the English that compose my new family in Christ. Is the gospel message as conveyed in Scripture really a message of truth? Is it true that sin has been put to death on the cross? Is it true that peace is possible between races? Unless the gospel of Jesus Christ is true, we all profess Christ in vain and there is no hope for us individually and corporately. I discovered that if I am to genuinely believe that I am saved by the cross, then I must also believe I am saved from my former life of sin for a life marked by God's righteousness. My prejudices against all those who mocked me and made me feel inferior through verbal and physical abuse and silent disdain come to an end at the cross.

Works Cited

Baird, William. *History of New Testament Research.* Volume 1: *From Deism to Tübingen;* volume two: *From Jonathan Edwards to Rudolf Bultmann*; volume 3: *From C. H. Dodd to H. D. Betz.* Minneapolis: Fortress, 1992-2013.

Balla, Peter. *Challenges to New Testament Theology: An Attempt to Justify the Enterprise.* Wissenschaftliche Untersuchungen zum Neuen Testament 95. Tübingen: Mohr Siebeck, 1997.

_____. *The Child-Parent Relationship in the New Testament and Its Environment.* Wissenschaftliche Untersuchungen zum Neuen Testament 155. Tübingen: Mohr Siebeck, 2014.

Barrett, Matthew. 'Is Our Doctrine of Inerrancy Christological Enough? The Future of Inerrancy and the Necessity of Dogmatics.' *Presbyterion* 44 (Spring 2018) pp. 25-41.

Bauckham, Richard. *The Gospel for All Christians.* Grand Rapids: Eerdmans, 1998.

Baur, F. C. *History of Christian Dogma.* Ed. Peter C. Hodgson, trans. Robert F. Brown and Peter C. Hodgson. Oxford: University Press, 2016 [original 1858].

_____. *Lectures on New Testament Theology.* Ed. Peter C. Hodgson, trans. Robert F. Brown. Oxford: University Press, 2016 [original 1864].

Bauspiess, Martin, Christof Landmesser, and David Lincicum, eds. *Ferdinand Christian Baur und die Geschichte des frühen Christentums.* Wissenschaftliche Untersuchungen zum Neuen Testament 333. Tübingen: Mohr Siebeck, 2014.

Benedict, Pope XVI. *Jesus of Nazareth.* Vol. 1: *Jesus of Nazareth: From the Baptism in the Jordan to the Transfiguration*; vol. 2 *Jesus of Nazareth: Holy Week: From the Entrance Into Jerusalem to The Resurrection*; vol. 3 *Jesus of Nazareth: The Infancy Narratives.* San Francisco: Ignatius Press, 2007–2012.

Benoit, Gregory C. *The Kingdom Unleashed: How Jesus' 1ˢᵗ-Century Kingdom Values Are Transforming Thousands of Cultures and Awakening His Church.* Murfreesboro, TN: DMM Library, 2018.

Berger, Klaus. *Die Bibelfälscher. Wie wir um die Wahrheit betrogen werden.* Neukirchen-Vluyn: Neukirchener Theologie, 2012.

Bird, Michael. Review of *Beyond Biblical Theology: Sacralized Culturalism in Heikki Räisänen's Hermeneutics. Review of Biblical Literature* 9 (2016).

Blomberg, Craig. 'A Constructive Traditional Response to New Testament Criticism.' In James K. Hoffmeier and Dennis R. Magary, eds., *Do Historical Matters Matter for Faith? A Critical Appraisal of Modern and Postmodern Approaches to Scripture.* Wheaton: Crossway, 2012. pp. 345-65.

—————. *The Historical Reliability of the New Testament: Countering Challenges to Evangelical Christian Beliefs.* Nashville: B&H Academic, 2016.

—————. *A New Testament Theology.* Waco, TX: Baylor University Press, 2018.

Bockmühl, Klaus. *The Unreal God of Modern Theology: Bultmann, Barth, and the Theology of Atheism.* Colorado Springs, CO: Helmers & Howard Publishers, 1988.

Bottum, Joseph. *An Anxious Age: The Post-Protestant Ethic and the Spirit of America.* New York: Image, 2014.

Bultmann, Rudolf. *Theology of the New Testament.* 2 vols. Trans. Kendrick Grobel. New York: Charles Scribner's Sons, 1951.

Cara, Robert. *Cracking the Foundation of the New Perspective on Paul: Covenantal Nomism versus Reformed Covenantal Theology.* Fearn, Ross-shire, U.K.: Christian Focus/Mentor, 2017.

Carlson, Darren. 'Christian Faith and Practice Amongst Migrants in Athens, Greece.' PhD thesis. Middlesex University. 2018.

Carson, D. A., ed. *The Enduring Authority of the Christian Scriptures*. Grand Rapids/Cambridge, U.K.: Eerdmans, 2016.

Chester, Stephen J. *Reading Paul with the Reformers: Reconciling Old and New Perspectives*. Grand Rapids: Eerdmans, 2017.

Cochlovius, Joachim and Peter Zimmerling, eds. *Evangelische Schriftauslegung: Ein Quellen- und Arbeitsbuch für Studium und Gemeinde*. Krelingen: Geistliches Rüstzentrum/Wuppertal: R. Brockhaus, 1987.

Congdon, David. *The God Who Saves: A Dogmatic Sketch*. Eugene, OR: Cascade, 2016.

_____. *The Mission of Demythologizing: Rudolf Bultmann's Dialectical Theology*. Minneapolis: Fortress, 2015.

Croy, N. Clayton. Review of Candida Moss, *The Myth of Persecution: How Early Christians Invented a Story of Martyrdom*. *Review of Biblical Literature* 10 (2013) 1-6.

Cummings, Brian. 'Luther in the Berlinka.' *Times Literary Supplement*, December 12, 2017.

Dorrien Gary. *Kantian Reason and Hegelian Spirit: The Idealistic Logic of Modern* Theology. Chichester, West Sussex, U.K.: Wiley-Blackwell, 2012.

Eskola, Timo. *Beyond Biblical Theology: Sacralized Culturalism in Heikki Räisänen's Hermeneutics*. Biblical Interpretation 123. Leiden: Brill, 2013.

Fesko, J. V. *The Spirit of the Age*. Grand Rapids: Reformation Heritage Books, 2017.

Frey, Jörg. *Von Jesus zur neutestamentlichen Theologie: Kleine Schriften II*. Ed. B. Schliesser. Wissenschaftliche Untersuchungen zum Neuen Testament 368. Tübingen: Mohr Siebeck, 2016.

Gadenz, Pablo T. 'Magisterial Teaching on the Inspiration and Truth of Scripture: Precedents and Prospects.' *Letter & Spirit* 6 (2010) pp. 67-91.

Gerdmar, Anders. 'The End of Innocence: On Religious and Academic Freedom and Intersubjectivity in the Exegetical Craft – A Response to James Kelhoffer.' *Svensk Exegetisk Årsbok* 82 (2017) pp. 179-209.

_____. *Rethinking the Judaism-Hellenism Dichotomy: A Historiographical Case Study of 2 Peter and Jude.* Coniectanea Biblica, New Testament Series 36. Stockholm: Almqvist & Wiksell, 2001.

_____. *Roots of Theological Anti-Semitism: German Biblical Interpretation and the Jews, from Herder and Semler to Kittel and Bultmann.* Studies in Jewish History and Culture 20. Leiden/ Boston: Brill, 2010.

_____ with Kari Syreeni. *Vägar till Nya Testamentet. Tekniker, metoder och verktyg för nytestamentlig exegetik.* Lund: Studentlitteratur, 2006.

Guthrie, Donald. *New Testament Theology.* Leicester, U.K. and Downers Grove, IL: Inter-Varsity, 1981.

Hammann, Konrad. *Rudolf Bultmann: A Biography.* Trans. Philip E. Devenish. Salem, OR: Polebridge, 2012.

_____. *Rudolf Bultmann – Eine Biographie.* Tübingen: Mohr Siebeck, 2009.

_____. *Rudolf Bultmann und seine Zeit: Biographische und theologische Konstellationen.* Tübingen: Mohr Siebeck, 2016.

Hardy, Nicholas. *Criticism and Confession: The Bible in the Seventeenth Century Republic of Letters.* Oxford: Oxford University Press, 2017.

Hartog, Paul. A., ed. *Orthodoxy and Heresy in Early Christian Contexts: Reconsidering the Bauer Thesis.* Eugene, OR: Pickwick, 2015.

Hatch, Nathan O. *The Democratization of American Christianity.* New Haven and London: Yale University Press, 1989.

Hedrick, Charles. 'The Church's Gospel and the Idiom of Jesus.' *The Fourth R* 30/4 (2017) pp. 3-7, 26.

Jenkins, Philip. *The New Faces of Christianity: Believing the Bible in the Global South.* New York: Oxford University Press, 2008.

_____. *The Next Christendom: The Coming of Global Christianity.* Third ed. New York: Oxford University Press, 2012.

Johnson, Todd M., Gina A. Zurlo, Albert W. Hickman, and Peter Crossing. 'Christianity 2017: Five Hundred Years of Protestant Christianity.' *International Bulletin of Missionary Research* 41/1 (January 2017) pp. 41-52.

_____. 'Christianity 2018: More African Christians and Counting Martyrs.' *International Bulletin of Missionary Research* 42/1 (January 2018) pp. 20-28.

_____. 'Christianity 2019: What's Missing? A Call for Further Research.' *International Bulletin of Missionary Research* 43/1 (January 2019) pp. 92-102.

Johnstone, Patrick. *The Future of the Global Church.* Downers Grove: InterVarsity, 2011.

Keith, Chris. *Jesus Against the Scribal Elite: The Origins of the Conflict.* Grand Rapids: Baker Academic, 2014.

Kelhoffer, James A. *Conceptions of 'Gospel' and Legitimacy in Early Christianity.* Wissenschaftliche Untersuchungen zum Neuen Testament 324. Tübingen: Mohr Siebeck, 2014.

_____. *The Diet of John the Baptist: Locusts and Wild Honey in Synoptic and Patristic Interpretation.* Wissenschaftliche Untersuchungen zum Neuen Testament 176. Tübingen: Mohr Siebeck, 2005.

_____. 'A Diverse Academy Recognizes No Boundaries for Critical Inquiry and Debate: A Rejoinder to Anders Gerdmar.' *Svensk Exegetisk Årsbok* 82 (2017) pp. 210-22.

_____. *Persecution, Persuasion, and Power: Readiness to Withstand Hardship As a Corroboration of Legitimacy in the New Testament.* Wissenschaftliche Untersuchungen zum Neuen Testament 270. Tübingen: Mohr Siebeck, 2010.

_____. 'Simplistic Presentations of Biblical Authority and Christian Origins in the Service of Anti-Catholic Dogma: A Response to Anders Gerdmar.' *Svensk Exegetisk Årsbok* 82 (2017) pp. 154-78.

Köstenberger, Andreas J. and Michael J. Kruger. *The Heresy of Orthodoxy: How Contemporary Culture's Fascination with Diversity Has Reshaped Our Understanding of Early Christianity.* Wheaton: Crossway, 2010.

Kümmel, W. G. *The New Testament: The History of the Investigation of its Problems*. Nashville: Abingdon, 1972.

Labron, Tim. *Bultmann Unlocked*. London: T&T Clark, 2011.

Ladd, George. *A Theology of the New Testament*. Rev. ed. Grand Rapids: Eerdmans, 1993.

Landmesser, Christof, ed. *Bultmann Handbuch*. Handbücher Theologie. Tübingen: Mohr Siebeck, 2017.

Legaspi, Michael. *The Death of Scripture and the Rise of Biblical Studies*. Oxford: Oxford University Press, 2011.

Leith, John H. *Crisis in the Church: The Plight of Theological Education*. Louisville: Westminster John Knox, 1997.

Lillback, Peter A. and Richard B. Gaffin, Jr. *Thy Word Is Still Truth: Essential Writings on the Doctrine of Scripture from the Reformation to Today*. Phillipsburg, PA: P&R, 2013.

Mahoney, Daniel J. *The Idol of Our Age: How the Religion of Humanity Subverts Christianity*. New York/London: Encounter Books, 2018.

Marshall, I. Howard. *New Testament Theology*. Downers Grove: IVP Academic, 2014.

Marty, Martin. *Dietrich Bonhoeffer's* Letters and Papers from Prison*: A Biography*. Princeton and Oxford: Princeton University Press, 2011.

Mathews, Kenneth A. and M. Sydney Park. *The Post-Racial Church: A Biblical Framework for Multiethnic Reconciliation*. Grand Rapids: Kregel, 2011.

Merk, Otto. *Biblische Theologie des Neuen Testaments in ihrer Anfangszeit: Ihre methodischen Probleme bei Johann Philipp Gabler und Georg Lorenz Bauer und deren Nachwirkungen*. Marburg: N. G. Elwert, 1972.

Moore, Stephen D. and Yvonne Sherwood. *The Invention of the Biblical Scholar: A Critical Manifesto*. Minneapolis: Fortress, 2011.

Moss, Candida. *The Myth of Persecution: How Early Christians Invented a Story of Martyrdom*. San Francisco: HarperOne, 2013.

Neill, Stephen and Tom Wright. *The Interpretation of the New Testament 1861–1986*, 2d ed. Oxford: Oxford University Press, 1988.

Noll, Mark. *The New Shape of World Christianity: How American Experience Reflects Global Faith*. Downers Grove: IVP Academic, 2013.

Nüssel, Freiderike. 'Kähler, Martin.' *Encyclopedia of the Bible and Its Reception*. Berlin/Boston: De Gruyter, 2017. Cols. 1221-2.

Oden, Thomas C. *A Change of Heart: A Personal and Theological Memoir*. Downers Grove: IVP Academic, 2014.

————. *Requiem: A Lament in Three Movements*. Nashville: Abingdon, 1995.

Pagels, Elaine. *Beyond Belief: The Secret Gospel of Thomas*. New York: Random House, 2003.

Park, M. Sydney. *A Biblical Theology of Women*. London: T & T Clark, 2019.

Patte, Daniel. *Ethics of Biblical Interpretation*. Louisville: Westminster/John Knox, 1995.

Priest, Robert J. and Kirimi Barine, eds. *African Christian Leadership: Realities, Opportunities, and Impact*. Maryknoll, NY: Orbis, 2017.

Qureshi, Nabeel. *No God But One: Allah or Jesus? A Former Muslim Investigates the Evidence for Islam and Christianity*. Grand Rapids: Zondervan, 2016.

————. *Seeking Allah, Finding Jesus: A Devout Muslim Encounters Christianity*. Expanded edition. Grand Rapids: Zondervan, 2016.

Romey, Kristen. 'The Search for the Real Jesus.' *National Geographic*, Dec. 2017 (232/6) pp. 30-69.

Sanneh, Lamin. *Summoned from the Margin: Homecoming of an African*. Grand Rapids/Cambridge, U.K.: Eerdmans, 2012.

————. *Whose Religion Is Christianity? The Gospel beyond the West*. Grand Rapids/Cambridge, U.K.: Eerdmans, 2003.

Schnabel, Eckhard J. 'The Persecution of Christians in the First Century.' *Journal of the Evangelical Theological Society* 61.3 (2018) pp. 525-47.

Schreiner, Thomas. *New Testament Theology*. Grand Rapids: Baker Academic, 2008.

Snodgrass, Klyne. 'Are the Parables Still the Bedrock of the Jesus Tradition?' *Journal of the Study of the Historical Jesus* 15/1 (2017) pp. 131-46.

Stuhlmacher, Peter. *Biblical Theology of the New Testament*. Trans. Daniel P. Bailey. Grand Rapids: Eerdmans, 2018.

_____. 'Die Tübinger Biblische Theologie des Neuen Testaments – ein Rückblick.' *Theologische Beiträge* 48 (2017) pp. 76-91.

Sundquist, Scott W. *The Unexpected Christian Century: The Reversal and Transformation of Global Christianity, 1900-2000*. Grand Rapids: Baker Academic, 2015.

Thielman, Frank. *Theology of the New Testament*. Second ed. Grand Rapids: Zondervan, 2015.

Tietz, Christiane. 'Karl Barth and Charlotte von Kirschbaum.' *Theology Today* 74/2 (2017) pp. 86-111.

Warfield, B. B. *The Works of Benjamin B. Warfield*. 10 vols. New York: Oxford University Press, 1932.

Wilckens, Ulrich. *Historische Kritik der historisch-kritischen Exegese: Von der Aufklärung bis zur Gegenwart*. Göttingen: Vandenhoeck & Ruprecht, 2017.

Wills, Gregory A. *Southern Baptist Seminary 1859–2009*. Oxford: Oxford University Press, 2009.

Witherington III, Ben. *The Indelible Image*. 2 vols. Downers Grove: InterVarsity, 2009-2010.

Woodbridge, John D. *Biblical Authority: A Critique of the Rogers/McKim Proposal*. Grand Rapids: Zondervan, 1982.

_____. 'Evangelical Self-Identity and the Doctrine of Biblical Inerrancy.' In Andreas Köstenberger and Robert Yarbrough, eds. *Understanding the Times*. Festschrift for D. A. Carson. Wheaton: Crossway, 2010. pp. 104-38.

_____. 'The Fundamentalist-Modernist Controversy.' In *Evangelical Scholarship, Retrospects and Prospects*. Eds. Dirk R. Buursma, Katya Covrett, and Verlyn D. Verbrugge. Festschrift for Stanley N. Gundry. Grand Rapids: Zondervan, 2017. pp. 57-107.

_____. 'Sola Scriptura: Original Intent, Historical Development and Import for Christian Living.' *Presbyterion* 44/1 (Spring 2018) pp. 4-24.

Yarbrough, Robert W. 'Bye-bye Bible? Progress Report on the Death of Scripture.' *Themelios* 39/3 (November 2014).

_____. *'God's Word in Human Words*: Form-Critical Reflections.' In James K. Hoffmeier and Dennis R. Magary, eds., *Do Historical Matters Matter for Faith? A Critical Appraisal of Modern and Postmodern Approaches to Scripture*. Wheaton: Crossway, 2012. pp. 327-43.

_____. Review of *Ethics of Biblical Interpretation. JETS* 40/1 (March 1997) pp. 128-9.

_____. *The Salvation Historical Fallacy? Reassessing the History of New Testament Theology*. Leiden: Deo, 2004.

Zaspel, Fred G. *The Theology of B. B. Warfield: A Systematic Summary*. Wheaton: Crossway, 2010.

Links

Henry Center statement: http://henrycenter.tiu.edu/2018/01/a-modern-creature-introducing-a-conversation/

Jamie Schmidt martyrdom: https://www.lifesitenews.com/opinion/will-this-be-the-first-american-born-martyr

Lausanne Covenant: https://www.lausanne.org/content/covenant/lausanne-covenant

Le Peu on Sire: http://andyunedited.ivpress.com/2018/02/james_w_sire_1933-2018.php

Martha Myers martyrdom: https://www.samford.edu/news/2003/Slain-Missionary-Dr-Martha-Myers-Gave-Her-All-to-People-who-Were-Suffering

Martha Myers martyrdom update: https://www.imb.org/2017/12/15/martyrs-jibla-baptist-hospital/

A Reforming Christian Confession: https://reformingcatholicconfession.com/

Salzburg Declaration: http://www.ikbg.net/

Wilckens testimony (German): http://kath.net/news/50015

Scripture Index

Subject Index

Also available in the REDS series...

Death in Adam, Life in Christ

The Doctrine of Imputation

J. V Fesko

The doctrine of imputation is the ground in which salvation is rooted. It is often seen as superfluous or splitting hairs, and yet, without it, redemption automatically becomes reliant on our own works and assurance of salvation is suddenly not so sure. J. V. Fesko works through this doctrine looking at its long history in the church, its exegetical foundation, and its dogmatic formulation. In exploring imputed guilt from the First Adam alongside the imputed righteousness from the Second, this volume offers a helpfully well-rounded explanation of the doctrine.

Conversations over imputation are rarely informed by the history of interpretation. Fesko introduces us to seminal figures in this development and no engagement with original sin or justification should overlook his careful spade work.

Michael Horton
J. Gresham Machen Professor of Systematic Theology and Apologetics,
Westminster Seminary California, Escondido, California

In classic Reformed fashion, and with grace and style, John Fesko brings confessional exposition, historical survey, and exegesis together in what is sure to become the standard Reformed work on Imputation for generations to come.

Brian Vickers
Professor of New Testament Interpretation and Biblical Theology,
The Southern Baptist Theological Seminary, Louisville, Kentucky

978-1-7819-1908-8

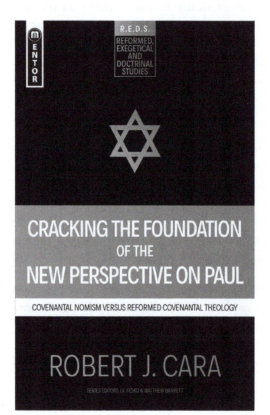

R.E.D.S.

REFORMED,
EXEGETICAL
AND
DOCTRINAL
STUDIES

CRACKING THE FOUNDATION

OF THE

NEW PERSPECTIVE ON PAUL

COVENANTAL NOMISM VERSUS REFORMED COVENANTAL THEOLOGY

ROBERT J. CARA

SERIES EDITORS J.V. FESKO & MATTHEW BARRETT

Cracking the Foundation of the New Perspective on Paul

Covenental Nomism versus Reformed Covenental Theology

ROBERT J. CARA

The New Perspective on Paul claims that the Reformed understanding of justification is wrong – that it misunderstands Paul and the Judaism with which he engages. The New Perspective's revised understanding of Second Temple Judaism provides the foundation to a new perspective. This important book seeks to show that this foundation is fundamentally faulty and cannot bear the weight it needs to carry, thus undermining the entirety of the New Perspective on Paul itself.

With impressive analysis of the historical sources, and careful attention to overlooked texts, Cara shakes the foundation of what seemed to be an unshakable system.

Michael J. Kruger
President and Professor of New Testament, Reformed Theological Seminary, Charlotte, North Carolina

Robert J. Cara's Cracking the Foundation of the New Perspective on Paul is a fresh response to one of the most vigorous challenges to the Reformation's doctrine of justification in the last quarter century. Students and scholars alike will benefit from this fair-minded and firm engagement.

Guy Prentiss Waters
James M. Baird, Jr. Professor of New Testament, Reformed Theological Seminary, Jackson, Mississippi

Robert Cara directs our attention to the primary sources, to what the texts themselves say. He writes in an engaging and accessible style, showing that a Reformational reading is faithful to Paul's theology.

Thomas R. Schreiner
James Buchanan Harrison Professor of New Testament Interpretation and Associate Dean,
The Southern Baptist Theological Seminary, Louisville, Kentucky

978-1-7819-1979-8

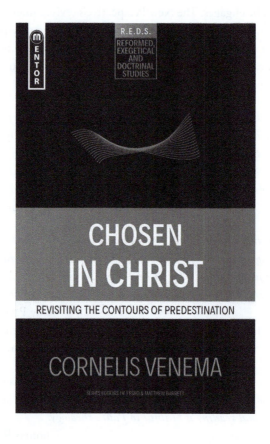

R.E.D.S.
REFORMED,
EXEGETICAL
AND
DOCTRINAL
STUDIES

CHOSEN
IN CHRIST

REVISITING THE CONTOURS OF PREDESTINATION

CORNELIS VENEMA

SERIES EDITORS J.V. FESKO & MATTHEW BARRETT

Chosen in Christ

Revisiting the Contours of Predestination

CORNELIS P. VENEMA

Cornel Venema revisits the important doctrine of predestination to re-familiarize the church with truths about God's sovereignty in salvation. But he does not merely re-visit old ground but also engages a host of historic and contemporary challenges to the doctrine. He addresses the subject from exegetical, historical, contemporary, and pastoral vantage points.

This is a magnificent discussion of predestination and election. I can think of no better resource, for not only does it address the usual questions surrounding this difficult but vital topic but it does so with close attention to the Biblical text and in dialogue with the history of thought from Augustine to the present day.

Robert Letham
Wales Evangelical School of Theology, Bridgend, Wales

This is an important book for the lucid and instructive treatment of predestination it provides. Composed of in-depth biblical, historical, and theological discussions with some concluding pastoral reflections, it will greatly benefit all who are interested in this doctrine and the crucial issues involved—issues, the author shows convincingly, that concern nothing less than the heart of the gospel.

Richard Gaffin
Professor of Biblical and Systematic Theology, Emeritus, Westminster Theological Seminary, Philadelphia, Pennsylvania

978-1-5271-0235-4

Also available from Christian Focus…

BRIAN CROFT &
JAMES B. CARROLL

FOREWORD BY MARK CLIFTON

FACING
SNARLS&
SCOWLS

PREACHING THROUGH
HOSTILITY, APATHY, AND ADVERSITY
IN CHURCH REVITALIZATION

Facing Snarls and Scowls

Preaching through Hostility, Apathy, and Adversity

BRIAN CROFT AND JAMES B. CARROLL

Pastor, the hard work of church revitalization is a unique experience and battle ground. It can feel like you're all alone. But the trials you face are not new. Faithful preachers throughout scriptures and church history have encountered hostility, apathy, and adversity, and continue to do so today. Brian Croft and James Carroll here share their personal stories and seek to encourage you to faithfully persevere in this Spirit–empowered, God–honoring, Christ–exalting work.

It seems I have read enough books on preaching to populate a small book store, but never one like this. Both authors have served as faithful preachers in a revitalizing context for many years and have long practiced the things they write about here. Read it and be reminded (and instructed) that the power of God for transformation—for the church—lies in what the apostle Paul calls 'the foolishness of preaching.'

Jeff Robinson
Pastor, Christ Fellowship Church of Louisville, Kentucky and Senior Editor, The Gospel Coalition

Despair, fatigue, and frustration are grave threats to pastoral ministry. How does one not only endure but improve as a preacher when there is little affirmation and few signs of growth? Here is a book that gives advice and inspiration for preachers who need encouragement to stay true to their calling to preach the Word (2 Tim. 4:1).

Joe Barnard
Founder, Cross Training Ministries

978-1-5271-0382-5

Christian Focus Publications

Our mission statement —

STAYING FAITHFUL

In dependence upon God we seek to impact the world through literature faithful to His infallible Word, the Bible. Our aim is to ensure that the Lord Jesus Christ is presented as the only hope to obtain forgiveness of sin, live a useful life and look forward to heaven with Him.

Our books are published in four imprints:

CHRISTIAN
FOCUS

Popular works including biographies, commentaries, basic doctrine and Christian living.

CHRISTIAN
HERITAGE

Books representing some of the best material from the rich heritage of the church.

MENTOR

Books written at a level suitable for Bible College and seminary students, pastors, and other serious readers. The imprint includes commentaries, doctrinal studies, examination of current issues and church history.

CF4•K

Children's books for quality Bible teaching and for all age groups: Sunday school curriculum, puzzle and activity books; personal and family devotional titles, biographies and inspirational stories — because you are never too young to know Jesus!

Christian Focus Publications Ltd,
Geanies House, Fearn, Ross-shire,
IV20 1TW, Scotland, United Kingdom.
www.christianfocus.com
blog.christianfocus.com